THE

# CHARTER OF THE CITY OF DETROIT,

(AS AMENDED,)

TOGETHER WITH

## ACTS OF THE LEGISLATURE

RELATING TO THE CITY,

WITH

## AN APPENDIX.

---

PRINTED BY ORDER OF THE COMMON COUNCIL.

DETROIT:

W. F. STOREY, CITY PRINTER, FREE PRESS MAMMOTH PRINTING HOUSE.

1861.

# CONTENTS OF CHAPTERS.

# CHARTER

OF

# THE CITY OF DETROIT.

---

[*No.* 55. *Laws of Michigan*, 1857.]

---

**AN ACT to Revise the Charter of the City of Detroit.**

[*Approved February 5th*, 1857.]

WITH THE AMENDMENTS CONTAINED IN THE FOLLOWING ACTS:

[*No.* 129. *Laws of* 1859. *Approved February* 12*th*, 1859]
[*No.* 252. *Laws of* 1859. *Approved February* 15*th*, 1859.]
[*No.* —. *Laws of* 1861. *Approved March* 12*th*, 1861.]

---

## CHAPTER I.

### INCORPORATION—CITY AND WARD BOUNDARIES.

SECTION
1. Incorporation; name and powers of the corporation; seal of.

SECTION
2. City boundaries established. Creation of Wards; their boundaries; how altered.

SECTION 1. *The People of the State of Michigan enact*, That the corporation heretofore created and now known as "The Mayor, Recorder, Aldermen and Freemen of the City of Detroit," shall be and continue to be a corporation by the name of "THE CITY OF DETROIT," and by that name may sue and be sued, implead and be impleaded, complain and defend, in any court of record, and in any other place whatsoever; may have a common seal and alter it at pleasure,

Corporation.

Name and powers of.

Seal of.

and may take, hold, purchase, lease, convey and dispose of any real, personal or mixed estate for the use of said corporation.

Boundaries.

SEC. 2. The district of country in the county of Wayne, and State of Michigan, hereinafter particularly described, is hereby constituted and declared to be a city, by the name of Detroit, and subject to the municipal government of said corporation, said district of country being bounded as follows, viz.: Beginning at a point on the national boundary line in the Detroit River, directly opposite and in a line with the dividing line between the Baker and Woodbridge farms, so called, and running thence north twenty-two degrees and forty-seven minutes west, to the margin of said river; thence north twenty-two degrees and forty-seven minutes west, along said dividing line to the rear or northerly line of the Baker farm aforesaid; thence north-easterly along the rear or northerly line of the Baker, Labrosse and Forsyth farms, so called, to the north-westerly corner of the Jones farm, so called; thence north sixty degrees east, on a course parallel with Jefferson avenue, to a point opposite the dividing line between the Dequindre and Witherell farms, so called; thence south twenty-six degrees east, to the north-easterly corner of the Dequindre farm aforesaid, being the north-western corner of the Witherell farm aforesaid; thence south twenty-six degrees east, along said line of said farms, to the margin of the Detroit River aforesaid; thence south twenty-six degrees east to the national boundary line in said river, and thence south-westerly along said national boundary line to the place of beginning.

Wards established—how altered.

The wards of said city shall be and remain as heretofore laid out and constituted, until altered by the Common Council of said city, as authorized by this act. (*See Act to enlarge City limits, post.*)

# CHAPTER II.

## OFFICERS—WHO ELECTED, WHO APPOINTED, QUALIFICATIONS, BONDS, OFFICIAL TERMS, REMOVAL, VACANCY.



SECTION 1. The following officers of the corporation shall be elected at the annual city election, on a general ticket, by the qualified electors of the whole city, viz.: Mayor, Recorder, City Clerk, Attorney, Treasurer, City Surveyor, and Director of the Poor. *Officers elected on general ticket.*

The following officers of the corporation shall be elected at said election on a ward ticket, in each ward, by the qualified electors thereof, viz.: Two Aldermen, two School Inspectors, a Collector, Overseer of Highways, and Constable. [*As amended by Section* 1 *of the Act of* 1861. *On ward ticket.*

Officers appointed by Common Council.

SEC. 2. The following officers shall be appointed by the Common Council, at a meeting to be held on the second Tuesday of January in each year, viz.: Superintendent of Alms House, a Sealer of Weights and Measures, a Clerk of the Recorder's Court, who shall be appointed on the recommendation of the Recorder, one or more Collectors, one or more Physicians, one or more Street Commissioners, a Marshal, one or more Assistant Marshals, one or more Clerks of the Markets, and such other officers, deputies, assistant officers and agents as may be necessary, and whose appointment shall be authorized by prior resolution of the Common Council. A Controller shall be appointed on the second Tuesday of March preceding the expiration of his term of office, and on the nomination of the Mayor, a Receiver of Taxes, whose term of office shall be two years; a Superintendent of the House of Correction, whose term of office shall be three years, and a Counselor, who shall be a practicing attorney, and whose term of office, duties and compensation shall be prescribed by the Common Council: *Provided*, That any appointment which shall not be made on the day named, may be made at any subsequent regular session of the Common Council: *And provided further*, That any office created by ordinance or resolution of the Common Council, may be filled at any time until the second Tuesday of January following, when, as in case of other officers, the regular term of service shall commence, and the office, if continued, be filled for the ensuing year, unless otherwise provided by the ordinance or resolution creating such office. [*As amended by Section* 2 *of the Act of* 1861.

Board of Water Commissioners.

SEC. 3. There shall also be the following boards of officers of the corporation, viz.: A Board of Water Commissioners, to be appointed and constituted as provided for in the act incorporating "The Board of Water Commissioners of the City of Detroit," approved February 14th, 1853; a

Board of Education.

Board of Education, to be constituted as provided for in the act incorporating "The Board of Education of the City of

Detroit," approved February 17th, 1842, and all acts amendatory thereto; and a Board of Inspectors of Election, to be appointed and constituted as hereinafter provided; and a Board of three Sewer Commissioners, who shall be appointed by the Common Council, on the nomination of the Mayor, and who shall appoint a competent Engineer, and, with his aid, it shall be their duty to propose a plan for constructing sewers and drains for the whole city—having reference, however, to the sewers and drains already constructed, or in process of construction—and said Board shall have such further powers and duties, in respect to the sewers and drains of said city, as said Common Council shall by ordinance prescribe. Said Commissioners shall receive no compensation for their services, shall hold their office for the term of five years, with the exception of the first Board, who shall hold their office for the respective terms of three, four, and five years, and the respective terms of each shall be determined by lot, under the direction of the City Attorney and Controller, and when thus determined, such determination shall be certified by said Attorney and Controller to the Common Council, and entered upon their journal, and such certificate shall be evidence of the respective term for which the several members of said Board have been elected. It shall be the duty of said engineer, under the direction of said Board, to superintend the construction and repair of sewers.

Board of Inspectors of Election.

Sewer Commissioners.

Engineer.

Sewers and Drains.

Commissioners to receive no compensation.

Term of Office.

Duties of Engineer.

SEC. 4. There shall be six Justices of the Peace in and for said city, who shall be elected on the general ticket at the annual city election in the same manner, shall hold their offices for the same terms and by the same tenure, possess the same jurisdiction and powers, subject to the act of the Legislature establishing a Police Court of the City of Detroit, and be subject to the same duties and liabilities, as provided by the general laws of this State in relation to the election, jurisdiction, powers, duties and liabilities of Justices of the Peace for townships; but the Justices of the Peace of said city, now in office, shall continue to hold their offices for

Justices of the Peace—their term of office, jurisdiction, powers and duties.

Justices now in office to continue.

the terms for which they have been elected, and in conformity to the general laws of this State: *Provided, however*, That at the election, to be held in April, 1857, a Justice of the Peace may be elected to fill the vacancy which will occur by the expiration of the term of such Justice, in July, 1857.

Proviso.

Officers to be residents of Detroit.

SEC. 5. No person shall be elected or appointed to, or shall hold any office under this act, who shall not be, at the time of his election, or appointment, and so long as he shall hold such office, a resident elector of said city; and no person shall be elected or appointed to, or shall hold office for any ward in said city, who at the time of his election or appointment, and so long as he shall hold such office, shall not be a resident elector of the ward from and for which he may be elected or appointed. If any person, elected or appointed to any office of the corporation, shall cease to be a resident of the city, or of the ward, for which he may have been elected or appointed, such office shall thereby be vacated: *Provided, however*, That a School Inspector shall not vacate his office by his removal from one ward to another ward in said city.

Proviso.

Qualificati'ns of Attorney.

SEC. 6. No person shall be elected to the office of Attorney, unless he be at the time of his election a Counselor of the Supreme Court of this State of two years' standing.

Defaulters ineligible.

SEC. 7. No person shall be elected or appointed to any office created by this act, who is now, or hereafter may be, a defaulter to said city, or to any board of officers thereof, or to the State of Michigan, or any county thereof; and any person shall be considered a defaulter who has refused, or neglected, or may hereafter refuse or neglect, for thirty days after demand made, to account for and pay over to the party authorized to receive the same, any public money which has come in his possession. If any person holding any such office shall become a defaulter, while in office, the same shall thereby be vacated.

Ignorance a disqualification for office

SEC. 8. No person shall be elected or appointed to any office under this act, except the offices of Scavenger and

Chimney Sweeper, unless he is able to read and write the English language intelligibly; and if any such person be elected or appointed, the Common Council shall declare such appointment or election void.

SEC. 9. No member of the Common Council shall, after his election, and during the time for which he was elected, or within one year thereafter, be appointed to any office under this act, which shall have been created, or the emoluments of which shall have been increased, during such time. Aldermen to hold no other office.

SEC. 10. No person interested, directly or indirectly, either as principal or surety, in any contract or agreement, written or verbal, to which the corporation shall be a party in interest, or to which any officer or board under this act shall officially be a party, for the construction of any sewer, pavement, building, or performance of any public work whatever, or for involving the expenditure, receipt or disposition of money or property of the corporation, Common Council, or by any officer or board under this act, shall be eligible or appointed to any office under this act; and if any person thus interested shall be elected or appointed to office, his election or appointment shall be void, and his office shall be deemed vacant. Persons interested disqualified for office.

SEC. 11. If any member of the Common Council, or other officer of the corporation, after his election or appointment, or while in office, shall become, or cause himself to become interested, directly or indirectly, in any contract or agreement, written or verbal, to which the corporation shall be a party in interest, or to which any officer or board under this act shall officially be a party, or in any question, subject or proceeding, pending before the Common Council, with intent to gain, directly or indirectly, any benefit, profit, or pecuniary advantage, he shall be removed from his office, and his office declared vacant by the Common Council, and he shall be deemed guilty of willful and corrupt malfeasance in office, and may be prosecuted therefor, and on con- Officers becoming interested to be removed.

Punishment. viction, shall be punished by a fine not exceeding one thousand dollars, or imprisonment in the State prison not exceeding one year, or both, at the discretion of the court.

Bribery. SEC. 12. If any person shall offer, directly or indirectly, to a member of the Common Council, or if any member of the Common Council shall directly or indirectly accept, or agree to accept, or receive any money, goods, or chattels, or any bank note, bank bill, bond, promissory note, due bill, bill of exchange, draft, order or certificate, or any security for the payment of money or goods and chattels, or any deed or writing containing a conveyance of land, or containing a transfer of any interest in real estate, any valuable contract, in force, or any other property or reward whatsoever, in consideration that such member of the Common Council will vote affirmatively or negatively, or that he will not vote, or that he will use his interest or influence on any question, ordinance, resolution, or other matter or proceeding pending before the Common Council, he shall be removed from office, and his office declared vacant by the Common Council, and both he and the person making such offer as aforesaid, shall be deemed guilty of misdemeanor, and may be prosecuted therefor, and on conviction, shall be punished by a fine not exceeding one thousand dollars, or imprisonment in the State prison not exceeding one year, or both, at the discretion of the court.

Punishment.

Terms of office. SEC. 13. The Water Commissioners shall hold their respective offices for the term of five years, the Controller and Superintendent of the House of Correction for the term of three years, the Recorder for the term of six years, the Mayor, Aldermen, School Inspectors, Treasurer, City Clerk, Attorney, Marshal, City Surveyor, Director of the Poor, and Receiver of Taxes for the term of two years, and all other officers who are elected or appointed, shall hold for the term of one year: *Provided*, *however*, That all officers, whether elected or appointed, shall hold their offices respectively until their successors shall be duly elected or appointed and

Proviso.

qualified, and shall enter upon the discharge of their duties. [*As amended by Section 3 of the Act of* 1861.

SEC. 14. The official terms of all officers who are elected, shall commence on the second Tuesday of January, after the annual city election at which they may have been elected, on which day there shall be a meeting of the Common Council; and the official terms of all officers who are appointed shall commence and expire on the third Tuesday of January, (on which day there shall also be a meeting of the Common Council,) except the Water Commissioners, whose official terms shall commence and expire as provided for in the act incorporating "The Board of Water Commissioners of the City of Detroit," approved February 14th, 1853, and the Controller, whose official term shall commence and expire on the first Tuesday in April. Commencement of Official Terms.

SEC. 15. Every officer, appointed or elected under this act, before entering on the duties of his office, shall take and subscribe the following oath of office: "I do solemnly swear (or affirm) that I will support the constitution of the United States and of this State, and that I will faithfully discharge the duties of such office to the best of my ability;" and shall file said oath, duly certified by the officer before whom it was taken, in the office of the Clerk of said city. Oath of Office

SEC. 16. Officers, who are elected at the annual city election, shall take and subscribe the oath of office before the City Clerk, file their official bonds, and enter upon their official duties, on the second Tuesday of January next ensuing their election, or within ten days thereafter; and officers who are appointed for full terms, shall take and subscribe the oath of office, file their official bonds, and enter upon their official duties on the third Tuesday of January, or within ten days thereafter; but officers who are either elected at a special election, or appointed to fill the unexpired portion of a term, shall take and subscribe the oath of office, file their official bonds, and enter upon their duties within ten days next ensu- Oaths, before whom taken.

ing notice of their election or appointment, except Justices of the Peace.

Discontinuing Office.

SEC. 17. Any office hereby authorized, but not specially named, may at any time be discontinued by the Common Council, and if there be an incumbent in such office, such discontinuance shall, on notice thereof, discharge him from the office and a further execution of its duties, and his office be deemed vacant.

Recorder subject to impeachm't.

SEC. 18. The Recorder shall be subject to impeachment and removal from office for corrupt conduct in office, or for crimes and misdemeanors, in the same manner as judicial officers, pursuant to the provisions of the constitution of this State.

Expulsion from Office.

SEC. 19. The Common Council may expel or remove from office any of its own members, or any other officer holding office by election, except the Mayor and Recorder, for corrupt or willful malfeasance or misfeasance in office, or for willful neglect of the duties of his office, by a vote of two-thirds of all the Aldermen elect, and in such case the reasons for such expulsion or removal shall be entered on the records of the Common Council, with the names and votes of the members voting on the question. No officer holding office by election shall be expelled or removed by said Common Council, unless first furnished with a copy of the charges in writing, and allowed to be heard in his defense, with aid of counsel, and for the purposes hereof the Common Council shall have power to issue subpœnas, to compel the attendance of witnesses and the production of papers, when necessary, and shall proceed, within ten days after service of a copy of the charges, to hear and determine upon the merits of the case. If such officer shall neglect to appear and answer to such charges, his default may be deemed good cause for removal from office.

Mayor may suspend Officers.

The Mayor shall have power to suspend or remove from office the Marshal, Street Commissioners, Deputy Marshal, Constables, Overseers of Highways and officers of the Police; and in case of such suspension or removal he shall report the same, with the reasons therefor, to the Common Council.

Removal of Officers.

SEC. 20. Any officer holding office by apppointment, unless otherwise provided by law or ordinance, may be removed at any time by the Common Council, without charges, and a trial thereof, by a vote of the majority of the Aldermen elect, except the Controller, Receiver of Taxes, and Superintendent of the House of Correction, who may be removed for the same causes and on the same proceedings as a member of the Common Council. [*As amended by Section 4 of the Act of* 1861.

Temporary Suspension from Office.

SEC. 21. Any officer holding office by election, except the Recorder, against whom charges shall be preferred, may be suspended from office by a majority vote of all the Aldermen elected, until such charges shall be heard and determined; and any officer holding office by appointment, may be suspended temporarily from office, at any time, by the like vote.

Vacancies.

SEC. 22. In case of expulsion or removal from office, death, resignation or permanent disability of any officer, his office shall thereby become vacant, and may be so declared by the Common Council.

Resignation.

SEC. 23. Resignations of office shall be made to the Common Council, in writing, and be subject to their approval and acceptance.

Filling vacancies in appointed offices.

SEC. 24. If any office of appointment shall become vacant, the Common Council may appoint a successor to serve for the unexpired portion of the official term.

Vacancies in office of Mayor or Aldermen; how filled.

SEC. 25. If a vacancy occurs in the office of Mayor or Alderman more than six months before the time for holding the next succeeding annual city election, the Common Council shall order a special election to fill such vacancy for the residue of the official term; if it occurs within six months before the time for holding such election, the Common Council may, in its discretion, order a special election to fill such vacancy for the residue of the official term.

Vacancies in other elective offices; how filled.

SEC. 26. If a vacancy occurs in any elective office, other than that of Mayor, Recorder or Alderman, the Common Council shall appoint some person, eligible under this act, to serve in such office until the next annual election, when the vacancy shall be filled for the residue of the official term.

Official bonds

SEC. 27. The Controller, Treasurer, Clerk, Attorney, Receiver of Taxes, Superintendent of the House of Correction, Collectors, Marshal, Clerk of the Markets, Street Commissioners, and Constables, shall, *respectively*, before they enter upon the duties of their respective offices, and such other officers as the Common Council may direct, file in the Clerk's office an official bond, in such sum and with such sureties as the Common Council shall direct and approve. *As amended by Section* 5 *of the Act of* 1861.

Condition of Official Bonds.

SEC. 28. The official bond of every officer shall be conditioned that he will faithfully perform the duties of his office, and will, on demand, deliver over to his successor in office, or other proper officer or agent of the corporation, all books, papers, moneys, effects and property belonging to the corporation, or appertaining to his office, which may be in his custody as an officer; and such bond may be further conditioned as the Common Council shall prescribe. The official bond of every officer whose duty it may be to receive or pay out money, besides being conditioned as above required, shall be further conditioned that he will, on demand, pay over or account for to the corporation, or any proper officer or agent thereof, all moneys received by him as such officer.

Constables' Bonds.

SEC. 29. Every person elected to the office of constable in said city, before entering on the duties of his office, shall, with two or more sureties, to be approved by the Common Council, execute and file with the City Clerk a bond or instrument, in writing, to the City of Detroit, in the penal sum of two thousand dollars, conditioned well and faithfully in all things, to execute and perform the duties of his office during the continuance therein, and to pay to each and every

Condition.

person who may be entitled thereto, all sums of money which said constable may become liable to pay on account of any execution or process for the collection of money which shall be delivered to him; and further conditioned as the Common Council may prescribe. [*As amended by Section* 6 *of the Act of* 1861.

Renewal of Official Bonds.

SEC. 30. The Common Council may at any time require any officer, whether elected or appointed, to execute and file with the Clerk of the city new official bonds in the same or in such further sums, and with new or such further sureties as said Council may deem requisite for the interest of the corporation.

Notice of Election to Office.

SEC. 31. The Clerk of the city shall cause every officer, whether elected or appointed, as soon as practicable after his election or appointment, to be served with a written notice thereof and of the amount of his official bond; and if such officer shall neglect to take and subscribe his oath of office, or to file his required official bond within the time prescribed therefor by this act; or if any officer, required to execute and file a new official bond, as provided in the preceding section, shall not comply with such requirement within ten days after notice thereof from the City Clerk, the Common Council may declare the office in such case vacant, and such vacancy may be filled as heretofore provided in this act.

Neglect to qualify.

Sureties in Official Bonds may be required to justify on Oath.

SEC. 32. The Common Council, or such officer as the Common Council shall by resolution or ordinance prescribe, may examine into the sufficiency of the proposed sureties in any official bond, or instrument, in writing, required by this act, or in any contract, in writing, to which the corporation or any officer or board under this act shall be a party in interest, and may require such sureties to submit to an examination, under oath, as to their property and responsibility. The depositions of the surety shall be reduced to writing, be signed by him, certified by the person taking the same, and annexed to and filed with the bond, or instrument in writing, to which it relates.

City Clerk to report delinquents to Council.

SEC. 33. The Clerk of the city shall report the name of any person elected or appointed to any office, who shall have neglected to file his official bond and oath of office, as required by this act, to the Common Council, at its next meeting after such default.

Aldermen may exercise powers of policemen.

SEC. 34. The aldermen of said city shall, by virtue of their office, be vested with, and may exercise all the powers of Policemen of said city. [*As amended by Section* 7 *of the Act of* 1861.

---

# CHAPTER III.

## ELECTIONS—HOW CONDUCTED.



Annual city election; time, place, and notice.

SECTION 1. The annual city election shall be held on the first Tuesday after the first Monday of November in each year, at such places in the several wards as shall be designated by an order of the Common Council, at least twenty days previous thereto, notice of which, specifying, also, the officers to be elected and the time for opening and closing the polls, shall immediately, or within three days after the date of such order, be given by the City Clerk, by publication in two or more daily newspapers published in said city. The time and place for holding a special election shall be designated, and the notice thereof given in the same manner, and to the same effect. Special elections.

SEC. 2. Each ward shall be an election district by itself; but it shall be lawful for the Common Council, in its discretion, at any time before the first day of October next preceding any charter or general election, to divide the several wards of the city, or either of them, into convenient election districts for the holding of general and special elections; and in case any ward or wards shall be so divided, the provisions of the general laws of the State, and of this act, relating to elections other than in towns, shall be applicable to such election districts. The Common Council shall, at least twenty days prior to any general or special election, appoint two Inspectors of Election for each ward so divided into election districts, and one of the Inspectors so appointed, with one of the Aldermen of the ward so divided, shall act as a Board of Registration in each of said election districts; and with one Inspector to be elected by a *viva voce* vote of the electors of the district, on the opening of the polls at any election, shall form a Board of Inspectors for said election. Vacancies in any Board of Inspectors, may be filled by the electors present, as in other cases of such vacancies. Any election district so made, shall remain an election district by itself until changed by the Common Council. Every elector shall vote in the ward and district in which he resides, as provided by law. The residence of an elector shall be the ward and district in which his family resides, or in which is his regular boarding house. [*As amended by Section* 8 *of the Act of* 1861. Council may divide wards into election districts. Inspectors; how appointed. Board of Registration. Board of Inspectors. Where electors shall vote. Residence defined.

SEC. 3. At every election, the Inspectors of Election for the ward or district in which such election may be held, in case the ward has not been divided into election districts, shall consist of the Aldermen of the ward and a third person, Inspectors of election.

to be chosen *viva voce* by the electors present, from their number, at the time of opening the polls; and in case the ward has been divided into election districts, the Inspectors of Election shall consist of one Alderman of the ward, one of the persons appointed by the Common Council for that purpose, and one elector of the ward and district, chosen by a *viva voce* vote of the electors present, at the time of opening the polls; and if, from any cause, either or both of the Aldermen, or of the Inspectors appointed by the Common Council, shall fail to attend such election, his or their places shall be supplied by the electors present, who shall elect any of their number *viva voce*. Said Inspectors, before entering upon their duties, shall each take the same oath of office prescribed for other officers under this act. [*As amended by Section* 9 *of the Act of* 1861.

Oath of Inspectors.

Clerks of election; how appointed.

SEC. 4. The Inspectors of each ward, if not divided into election districts, and in each district, if so divided, shall appoint two competent Clerks of the election, who shall take the same oath as the Inspectors, which oath either of the Inspectors may administer. [*As amended by Section* 10 *of the Act of* 1861.

Ballot box.

SEC. 5. One suitable ballot box, with lock and key, shall be provided and kept by the City Clerk, at the expense of the city, for each ward or district; and it shall be the duty of the City Clerk to deposit such box, with the key, in the hands of the Inspectors of each ward or district, prior to the opening of the polls. [*As amended by Section* 11 *of the Act of* 1861.

Opening and closing polls.

SEC. 6. The polls of election shall be opened at eight o'clock in the forenoon, or as soon thereafter as may be, on the day of election, and shall be continued open until five o'clock in the afternoon of the same day, and no longer.

Qualification of voters.

SEC. 7. The qualifications of electors, under this act, shall be those prescribed in the first section of the seventh article of the constitution of this State, which is as follows:

"In all elections, every white male citizen, every white male inhabitant residing in the State on the twenty-fourth day of June, one thousand eight hundred and thirty-five; every white male inhabitant residing in this State on the first day of January, one thousand eight hundred and fifty, who has declared his intention to become a citizen of the United States, pursuant to the laws thereof, six months preceding an election, or who has resided in this State two years and six months, and declared his intention as aforesaid, and every civilized male inhabitant, of Indian descent, a native of the United States, and not a member of any tribe, shall be an elector, and entitled to vote; but no citizen or inhabitant shall be an elector, or entitled to vote at any election, unless he shall be above the age of twenty-one years, and has resided in this State three months, and in the township or ward in which he offers to vote, ten days next preceding such election."

SEC. 8. If, at any election, a vote shall be challenged, either of the Inspectors of Election shall be authorized to swear or affirm the person whose vote is challenged, to answer such questions as may be put to him touching his qualifications as an elector, and said Inspectors shall decide from such examination as to the legality of such vote. Challenge and oath.

SEC. 9. If any person, thus sworn or affirmed, shall willfully swear or affirm falsely, as to any material matter concerning his qualifications as an elector of said city, he shall be deemed guilty of perjury, and may be prosecuted therefor; and, on conviction thereof, be punished by a fine not exceeding one thousand dollars, or imprisonment at hard labor in the State prison for a period not exceeding five years, or both, in the discretion of the court. Perjury. Punishment.

SEC. 10. If any person shall vote in more than one ward or district, or more than once in the same ward or district, at any election in said city, he may be prosecuted therefor, and, on conviction, shall be punished by a fine not exceeding five hundred dollars, or imprisonment at hard labor in the State Punishment for voting more than once.

prison for a period not exceeding three years, or both, in the discretion of the court. [*As amended by Section* 12 *of the Act of* 1861.

Conducting elections.

SEC. 11. The manner of conducting and voting at elections to be held under this act, the keeping of the poll lists, canvassing of the votes, certifying the returns, and all other proceedings connected with such elections, shall be the same, as nearly as may be, as is now, or hereafter may be provided for by the laws of this State, applicable to general State elections, except as may be otherwise provided in this act.

Certifying returns of election.

SEC. 12. On canvassing the votes, the Inspectors shall certify a full and true return thereof, under their hands, to the Clerk of the city, carefully sealed up, together with the poll lists and ballots, within seventy-two hours after the closing of the polls; and the Inspectors of each election district shall thereupon choose one of their number to represent such election district, in the Board of City Canvassers, and the persons so chosen shall form the Board of Canvassers for the city, and shall, on the Saturday next after election, at three o'clock in the afternoon, meet at the City Clerk's office, or in the Common Council chamber, and proceed to open and canvass the said returns, and declare the result of the election. [*As amended by Section* 13 *of the Act of* 1861.

Canvass.

Conducting special elections.

SEC. 13. Special elections shall be conducted, as near as may be, in the same manner as general elections, but in such cases, the returns of the Inspectors shall be opened and canvassed, and the result declared by the Common Council, at its first meeting after the making of said returns.

Ballots for vacancy.

SEC. 14. If any person be voted for at any election, to fill a vacancy, or residue of a term, the ballots of the electors shall designate such vacancy, or residue.

To designate vacancy.

Plurality to elect.

SEC. 15. In the canvass of votes, any person who has received a plurality of the votes for any office, shall be declared duly elected to such office.

Proceedings in case of tie.

SEC. 16. When two or more persons shall have an equal number of votes for the same office, the election shall be determined by the drawing of lots in the presence of the Common Council. The names of each of such persons shall be written on separate slips of paper and deposited in a box, or other proper place, and the President of the Common Council shall draw out of said box, or other place, in the usual manner of determining by lot, one of said slips, and the person whose name is thereon, shall be deemed entitled to hold the office for which he received said votes, in the same manner as other officers duly elected.

Mode of conducti'g state, district, and county elections.

SEC. 17. The mode of conducting all State, district and county elections in said city, shall be in the manner herein provided for the election of city officers, except that the returns thereof shall be made to the County Clerk, and the same proceedings had, as near as may be, as are now or hereafter may be provided by law for the return of votes by township Inspectors of Election.

Privilege from arrest.

SEC. 18. No person, entitled to vote at any election held under this act, shall be arrested on civil process, within said city, on the day on which such election is held.

First election; time of.

SEC. 19. The first election, under this act, shall be held on the first Tuesday after the first Monday in November, 1857, and all officers now holding offices, by election, in said city, which are made elective by the people, under this act, shall continue to hold their respective offices until the second Tuesday of January, 1858. The Aldermen of said city, who were elected in the year 1855, shall continue in office until the second Tuesday in January, 1858, and shall be succeeded in office by the Aldermen who are elected in November, 1857, and the Aldermen who were elected in the year 1856, shall continue in office until the second Tuesday in January, 1859, and shall be succeeded in office by the Aldermen who are elected in November, 1858. In all cases where any new office is created, or where any vacancy may occur, under the provisions of this act, the Common Council may appoint persons to fill the same until the second Tuesday in January, 1858, when their successors shall be appointed, except the

Officers holding office to continue.

Assessor, who shall be appointed for his full term, as herein provided. The present Recorder of said city shall continue to hold his office until the second Tuesday in January, 1858, and shall possess and exercise the powers and duties now possessed and exercised by him, under the present charter of said city, and shall also be President of the Common Council, and shall possess and exercise the powers and duties of that office, as herein provided, until the expiration of his term of office, and shall receive such salary as the Common Council may prescribe. The present Controller of said city shall continue to hold his office until the first day of April, 1859. The office of Ward Assessor is hereby abolished.

---

# CHAPTER IV.

## OFFICERS—THEIR RIGHTS, POWERS AND DUTIES.



Mayor; his duty.

SECTION 1. The Mayor shall be the chief executive officer of the city of Detroit, and conservator of its peace. It shall be his duty to keep an office in some convenient place in said city, to be provided by the Common Council; to see that all officers of said city faithfully comply with and discharge their official duties; to see that all laws pertaining to the municipal government of said city, and all ordinances and resolutions of the Common Council be faithfully observed and executed; and he shall have power, in his discretion, to report to the Common Council any violations thereof. He shall, from time to time, give to the Common Council such information, and recommend such measures as he shall deem necessary or expedient.

Salary of Mayor.

SEC. 2. The Mayor shall be paid a salary of twelve hundred dollars *per annum*. In case of a vacancy in the office of Mayor, or of his being unable to perform the duties of his office, by reason of sickness, absence from the city, or other cause, the President of the Common Council shall be acting Mayor; and in case, at the same time, there shall also be a vacancy in the office of President of the Common Council, or he shall be unable to perform the duties of his office, by reason of sickness, absence from the city, or other cause, the President *pro tempore* of the Common Council shall be acting Mayor; and such acting Mayor shall be vested with all the powers, and shall perform all the duties of Mayor, until the vacancy or vacancies aforesaid be filled, or the Mayor or President of the Common Council, as the case may be, shall resume his office.

Who is to be acting Mayor in certain cases.

President of Common Council.

SEC. 3. The Common Council shall, at its first meeting in January in each year, select from their number a President for the year, and in case of a vacancy, or his temporary absence, supply his place by the election of a President *pro tempore*.

In certain cases President *pro tempore* to preside.

SEC. 4. The President *pro tempore* of the Common Council shall preside at its meetings, in case of a vacancy in the office of President of the Common Council, or of his being unable, from any cause, to be present and preside. In such case, the President *pro tempore* shall be invested with all the power, and shall perform all the duties, of President of the

Powers of.

Common Council, until he shall resume his office, or the vacancy therein be filled.

Duties of Attorney.

SEC. 5. The Attorney shall appear in and conduct all suits, prosecutions and proceedings in the Recorder's Court, to which the City of Detroit is a party, to the end thereof, subject to the rules and practice of said court, and if the same be removed to any other tribunal, by writ of error, habeas corpus, or otherwise, he shall conduct the case before such tribunal.

Duties of Clerk.

SEC. 6. The Clerk of the corporation shall keep the corporate seal, and all papers filed in or pertaining to his office, and shall be Clerk of the Common Council, shall attend its meetings, and shall make and preserve a record of all its ordinances, resolutions, and other proceedings, in proper books to be provided therefor, and when requested, shall duly certify, under the corporate seal, copies thereof, and of all papers duly filed in his office pertaining to the same, and shall possess and exercise the powers of Township Clerks.

Duties of Controller.

SEC. 7. It shall be the duty of the Controller to countersign all bonds which the corporation or Common Council is authorized to issue, pledging the faith and credit of said city; to receive all accounts and demands against the corporation, examine them in detail, audit and allow them, or such parts thereof as to the correctness of which he has no doubt, and which the claimant is willing to accept in full discharge thereof, file and number them as vouchers, in the order of their allowance, register them, with the amount allowed and date of allowance, in the same order, in a proper book provided for such purpose, and, on their being properly discharged, in writing, to draw and sign his warrant therefor, upon the Treasurer, when the same is ordered to be paid by the Common Council. If he shall have any doubt concerning their correctness, he shall register them in a separate list and return them to the Common Council, with his objections. If the same be allowed by the Common Council, in pursuance of their authority under this act, on

File vouchers.

Draw warrants.

Register doubtful accounts and return to Common Council.

their return to the Controller, with a certificate of the Clerk indorsed thereon that they have been allowed by the Common Council, he shall then file and register them in the list of allowed claims, in the same manner as above provided for the registering of claims audited and allowed by him, and, on their being properly discharged, in writing, shall draw and sign his warrant therefor on the Treasurer. It shall also be the duty of the Controller to lay before the Common Council, once in each year, in the month of April, or oftener if directed by the Common Council, a schedule of all accounts audited and allowed by him, and of all leases of the property of the corporation, specifying the names of the lessees, the rates of rent, and the period when the leases will terminate. It shall also be the duty of the Controller to examine the tax rolls and returns of the city officers, and take general supervision of the financial concerns of the corporation; to keep a complete set of books, exhibiting the financial condition of the corporation in its various departments and funds, its resources and liabilities, with a proper classification thereof, and each fund or appropriation for any distinct object of expenditure, or class of expenditures. When any such fund or appropriation has been exhausted by warrants already drawn thereon, or by appropriations, liabilities, debts, and expenses actually made, incurred, or contracted for, and to be paid out of such fund or appropriation, the Controller shall advise the Common Council thereof at its next meeting.

To present to Council schedule of accounts etc.

To examine tax rolls and returns of City Officers.

To advise Common Council when any fund is exhausted.

SEC. 8. The Controller shall also open an account with the Treasurer, in which he shall charge said Treasurer with the whole amount of taxes, general and special, levied in said city, also the whole amount in detail of all bonds, notes, mortgages, leases, rents, interest, and other moneys receivable, in order that the value and description of all personal property belonging to the corporation may, at any time, be known. He shall also keep a list of all the property, real, personal, and mixed, belonging to the corporation, and of all

To open an account with Treasurer.

To keep a list of property of corporat'n

its debts and liabilities, in order that the amount of the moneys and liabilities of the corporation may at any time be known at his office. The Controller shall also perform such other duties as are prescribed by this act, or may be prescribed by the Common Council, subject to the provisions hereof. The Controller shall also open accounts with the Treasurer, in which he shall charge him with all moneys appropriated, raised, or received for each of the several funds of the corporation, and credit him for all warrants drawn thereon, keeping a separate account of debit and credit for each fund, charging every warrant drawn to the account of the particular fund constituted or raised for the specific purpose for which such warrant is drawn, in order that it may be known, at the Controller's office, when each fund has been or may be exhausted, and what balance, if any, may remain therein.

SEC. 9. The Recorder, and the Clerk of the Recorder's Court, shall possess and exercise the powers and duties elsewhere prescribed in this act.

Duties of Treasurer.

SEC. 10. The Treasurer shall have the custody of all moneys, bonds, mortgages, notes, leases, and evidences of value belonging to the corporation. He shall receive all moneys belonging to and receivable by the corporation, and keep an accurate account of all receipts and expenditures thereof. He shall pay no money out of the Treasury, except in pursuance of and by authority of law, and on a warrant signed by the Controller, which shall specify the purpose for which the amount thereof is to be paid. He shall keep an accurate account of, and be charged with, all taxes and moneys appropriated, raised, or received for each fund of the corporation; shall keep a separate account for each fund, and shall pay every warrant out of the particular fund constituted or raised for the purposes for which said warrant was issued, and having the name of such fund indorsed thereon, by the Controller. He shall exhibit to the Common Council annually, and as often and for such period as may be required, a full and detailed account of all receipts and disbursements since the date of his last annual report, classifying them by the fund to which such receipts are credited, and out of which such disbursements are made; shall report to the Controller, at the end of each month, the amount received and credited by him to each fund, and on what account received; and shall also, when required, exhibit a general statement showing the financial condition of the treasury; which account, report, and statement shall be filed in the office of the Controller.

Sec. 11. The Marshal shall possess and exercise the powers and duties, as a conservator of the peace, which township constables, under the general laws of this State possess and may exercise, and shall possess and exercise such other powers and duties as shall be prescribed by the Common Council for the preservation of the public peace, and shall possess and exercise the same powers for the service and execution of all writs, process, and warrants issuing out of the Recorder's Court, in cases arising under the ordinances of the city, which sheriffs now have, or may have by law, for the service and execution of writs and process issuing from the Circuit Courts of this State. He shall obey and execute all lawful precepts and commands of said Common Council, and of said Recorder's Court; shall attend the sittings of said court, and he, or one of his deputies, shall attend the meetings of said Common Council. Powers and duties of Marshal.

Sec. 12. Assistant Marshals shall have and exercise the same powers and duties as the Marshal. Assistant Marshals.

Sec. 13. The Surveyor shall have power, and it shall be his duty, to survey within the corporation limits. He shall have the same power to make surveys and plats within the corporation limits, as are now or may hereafter be given, by law, to county surveyors, and the like effect and validity shall be given to his official acts, surveys, and plats, as are or may hereafter be given, by law, to the official acts, surveys, and plats of county surveyors. He shall make out the assess- Surveyor's powers and duties.

ment rolls for paving, for side and crosswalks, for lateral sewers, and for all other special assessments, and shall survey for the city.

Collector's duties.

SEC. 14. It shall be the duty of the Collector of the corporation to collect all special assessments imposed and levied by the Common Council, except such as shall be paid by the person assessed to the Receiver of Taxes, prior to the issue of the warrant for the collection of the same, as is or may be provided by the ordinances of said city. [*As amended by Section* 14 *of the Act of* 1861.

Assesor's duties.

SEC. 15. The Assessor shall assess all the property liable to assessment, for the purpose of levying the taxes lawfully imposed thereon, as hereinafter more particularly provided. The Assessor shall also prepare and return a list of persons to serve as jurors, as hereinafter provided in this act.

Street Commissioners to superintend construction and cleaning of pavem'ts, etc.

SEC. 16. The Street Commissioners, within their respective districts, under the direction of the Common Council, shall superintend the construction, repairs, and cleaning of pavements, sidewalks, crosswalks, culverts, and bridges, and direct the working, cleaning, and improving the highways, streets, alleys, and public places in said city. They shall keep an accurate record of the names of persons, together with the number of horses, carts, and wagons employed by them in the several wards, and render, under oath, to the Controller, a true account of the time of each, and the expenses thereof. [*As amended by Section* 15 *of the Act of* 1861.

Duties of Overseers of Highways.

SEC. 17. The Overseer of Highways for each ward shall, under the superintendence and control of the Street Commissioner, and when directed by him, work and improve the highways, streets, alleys, and public places of said city, in the ward for which he is elected: *Provided*, That nothing in this act contained shall be construed to prevent the Common Council, in its discretion, from paving, graveling, macadamizing, or otherwise improving and cleaning the streets, alleys, and public places of said city by contract; in which case such contract or contracts shall be awarded to the lowest qualified and responsible bidder, after due notice of the time of letting the same, in one or more of the daily newspapers published in said city. [*As amended by Section* 16 *of the Act of* 1861.

Duties of Ward Collectors.

SEC. 18. The Collector for each ward shall collect all State and county taxes assessed and imposed upon the real and personal property of such ward, and such city, highway, sewer, and school taxes as shall be placed in his hands for collection, by the Receiver of Taxes, or other proper officer of said city, and shall account for and pay over the same as required by law, or by ordinance, or resolution of the Common Council of said city. [*As amended by Section* 17 *of the Act of* 1861.

Books, etc., to be delivered to successors in office.

SEC. 19. Whenever any officer shall resign, or be removed from office, or the term for which he shall have been elected or appointed shall expire, he shall, on demand, deliver over to his successor in office all the books, papers, moneys, and effects in his custody, as such officer, and in any way appertaining to his office, and every person violating this provision, shall be deemed guilty of misdemeanor, and may be proceeded against in the same manner as public officers generally for the like offense, under the general laws of this State, now or hereafter in force and applicable thereto; and every officer, appointed or elected under this act, shall be deemed an officer within the meaning and provisions of such general laws of the State.

Penalties for violation.

General powers and duties of officers.

SEC. 20. In addition to the rights, powers, duties, and liabilities of officers prescribed in this act, all officers, whether elected or appointed, shall have such other rights, powers, duties, and liabilities, subject to and consistent with the provisions of this act, as the Common Council may deem expedient, and shall prescribe by ordinance or resolution.

Who may administer oath.

SEC. 21. The Mayor, Recorder, and members of the Common Council, Clerk, Controller, and Clerk of the Recorder's Court, are hereby authorized generally to administer oaths, and to take affidavits; but neither of said officers shall receive any fees therefor, except said clerks. The Controller shall have the power to take acknowledgments of deeds under the laws of this State.

Controller may take acknowledgm't of deeds.

Mayor may entertain complaints against persons to whom a license has been granted for violation of ordinances

SEC. 22. [*See note A.*] The Mayor may issue process, and hear, in a summary way, any complaint against any person to whom a license of any description has been granted in pursuance of this act, for any violation of the laws of the State, or the ordinances of the corporation, and may issue subpœnas and compel the attendance of witnesses, on the hearing of such complaint, in the same manner as Justices of the Peace, in the trial of civil cases, and on such hearing, may annul such license, or suspend it for any certain time. Every determination on such complaint shall be forthwith filed with the Clerk of the city, who shall serve a certified copy thereof on the person holding a license, affected by such determination, either personal, or by leaving the same at his or her usual place of abode; and from the time of such service, such license shall be annulled or suspended, according to the tenor of such determination.

Chairmen of committees may administer oaths respecting matters pending before them.

SEC. 23. [*See note A.*] The chairman of any committee, or special committee, or of any board established by this act, may administer any oath, or take any affidavit in respect to any matter pending before them respectively.

Unsafe buildings; powers of Council.

SEC. 24. [*See note A.*] Whenever, in the opinion of the Common Council, any building, fence, or other erection of any kind, or any part thereof, is liable to fall down and endanger persons or property, they may order any owner or occupant of the premises on which such building, fence, or other erection stands, to take down the same, or any part thereof, within such time as they may direct. In case the order be not complied with, they may cause the same to be taken down at the expense of the city, on account of the owner of the premises, and assess the expense on the land on which it stood. The order, if not immediate in its terms, may be served on any occupant of the premises, or be published in the city paper, as the Common Council shall direct.

SEC. 25. [*See note A.*] The Common Council shall audit and allow all accounts chargeable against the city; but no unliquidated account, or claim, or contract, shall be received for audit or allowance, unless it be accompanied with an affidavit of the person rendering it, to the effect that he verily believes that the services or property therein charged, have been actually performed or delivered for the city; that the sums charged therefor, are reasonable and just, and that, to the best of his knowledge and belief, no set-off exists, nor payment has been made on account thereof, except such as are included or referred to in such account or claim. It shall be a sufficient bar and answer to any action or proceeding, in any court, for the collection of any demand or claim against said city that it has never been presented to the Council for audit or allowance, or if on contract, that it was presented without said affidavit, and rejected for that reason, or that the action or proceeding was brought before the Council had a reasonable time to investigate and pass upon it.

Claims against city.

What sufficient bar to action against.

SEC. 26. The City Clerk shall countersign all licenses granted by the Mayor, or any other officer thereto authorized, and shall enter, in proper books, full minutes of all such licenses, and no license shall be valid unless so countersigned.

Clerk to countersign licenses.

---

NOTE A.—Sections 22, 23, 24, 25, and 26, were added to this Chapter by the Act of 1861.

# CHAPTER V.

## COMMON COUNCIL—POWERS AND DUTIES.



Who constitute the Common Council.

SECTION 1. The Aldermen of the city shall constitute the Common Council thereof, and a majority of all the Aldermen elected shall be a quorum for the transaction of business, but a smaller number may adjourn from day to day.

City Clerk to be clerk of.

SEC. 2. The Clerk of the city shall be Clerk of the Common Council.

Council to appoint President.

SEC. 3. The Common Council, at its first meeting after the annual city election, and after the newly elected Aldermen, or a majority thereof, shall have entered into their offices, shall appoint, by ballot, one of their number President, who shall serve until the first meeting of the Common Council after the next annual election, and until his successor be appointed, and shall have the powers and duties prescribed in this act.

Sessions of Council.

SEC. 4. The Common Council shall hold regular sessions at such times and places as they shall, by ordinance or resolution direct, and may adjourn regular sessions from time to time, as may be deemed expedient.

Special meetings; by whom called.

SEC. 5. Special meetings of the Common Council may be called at any time by the Mayor; or if one-third of all the Aldermen elected shall, in writing, request the President of the Common Council to call a special meeting, stating therein the time and objects thereof, and he shall refuse or neglect, for twenty-four hours, to call such meeting, a copy of such request to the President, may be filed with the Clerk of the city, with the certificate of any Alderman indorsed thereon, showing the presentation thereof to the President, and his refusal or neglect as aforesaid, and thereupon such special meeting shall be held, and the Clerk of the city shall cause notice thereof, and of its time and place, to be served on each of the members of the Common Council personally, or by leaving the same at their usual place of abode, and the proceedings of said meeting shall be limited to the objects thereof, as set forth in such request to the President. Special meetings may be adjourned from time to time, as may be deemed necessary, in order to dispose of the business which they are called to consider.

Notice of special meetings.

May be adjourned.

Ordinances and resolutions to be presented to Mayor for approval.

SEC. 6. Every ordinance, resolution, or proceeding of the Common Council, imposing taxes or assessments, or originating the expenditure or disposal of money or property, or whereby the corporation, or any board of officers under this act, may incur any debt or liability, and every ordinance and resolution, except resolutions making appointments to or removal from office, and except ordinances and resolutions for the fixing of salaries, and for the payment of debts and liabilities, previously and lawfully contracted, shall, before it takes effect, be presented by the Clerk to the Mayor. If the Mayor approve thereof, he shall thereon write his approval with the date thereof, and sign the same, and thereupon such ordinance, resolution, or proceeding shall go into effect; and such as he shall not so approve and sign, he shall return to the Common Council, with his objections thereto, in writing, under cover, sealed and addressed to said Common Council.

If Mayor approves, he shall write and sign his approval.

If Mayor shall not approve, he shall return with his objections.

Mayor's veto

SEC. 7. If the Mayor shall neglect to approve, as aforesaid, any ordinance, resolution, or proceeding, or return the same, as aforesaid, to said Common Council, with his objections, at its next regular meeeting after the same shall have been presented to him by the Clerk, as before provided, the same shall go into effect.

Reconsideration of veto'd resolutions, etc.

SEC. 8. Upon the return, as aforesaid, of any ordinance, resolution, or proceeding, the Common Council shall proceed to reconsider the vote by which the same was passed and adopted; and if, after such reconsideration, two-thirds of all the members elected shall agree by ayes and noes, which shall be entered of record, to pass or adopt the same, it shall go into effect.

Clerk's certificate of presentation.

SEC. 9. The Clerk of the city shall, at the time of presenting any ordinance, resolution, or proceeding of the Common Council to the Mayor, for his approval or disapproval, make a certificate, to be indorsed thereon or attached thereto, in which he shall specify the day on which the same was so presented; and such certificate shall be recorded with the proceedings of the Common Council.

Recording certificate.

Ordinances, etc., deposited with clerk and recorded

SEC. 10. All ordinances, resolutions, and written proceedings of the Common Council shall be deposited in the office of the Clerk of the city, who shall safely keep the same, and they shall be recorded in proper books, to be provided therefor. He shall keep a journal record of the proceedings of the Common Council, and also a record of every ordinance enacted, and of the time of its first publication, which record shall be signed by the Clerk, and by the President of the Common Council.

Clerk to keep journal and record.

Publication of proceedings.

SEC. 11. All proceedings of the Common Council shall be published in some daily newspaper published in said city. All ordinances shall be published for six successive days in the official daily newspaper of said city, and in one other daily newspaper published in said city, and shall take effect in ten days after their enactment: *Provided, however*, That the Common Council may fix and prescribe therein, a differ-

Proviso.

ent period, and that no ordinance shall take effect before at least one publication thereof.

SEC. 12. The style of ordinances shall be: "It is hereby ordained by the Common Council of the City of Detroit." Style of ordinances.

SEC. 13. All meetings of the Common Council shall be public, and its proceedings and records shall be open to public inspection, at reasonable times. Council meetings to be public.

SEC. 14. The inhabitants of said city shall have the right to petition the Common Council. Right of petition.

SEC. 15. The Common Council shall be the judge of the election and qualifications of its own members, and shall have the power to determine contested elections, to compel the attendance of absent members, to determine the rules of its proceedings, and pass all by-laws and rules necessary and convenient for the transaction of business, and not inconsistent with the provisions of this act. Council to be judge of qualification of its members.

SEC. 16. The Common Council shall have the general management and control of the finances, and all the property, real, personal, and mixed, belonging to the corporation, whether lying within or beyond the limits of said city, with full power to lease, sell, convey, transfer and dispose of the same absolutely; and shall have power to make all necessary regulations for preserving and protecting the same from destruction, decay, or injury, and concerning the management thereof. Council's powers over city property

SEC. 17. No resolution, ordinance, or proceeding of the Common Council, imposing taxes or assessments, or requiring the payment, expenditure, or disposal of money or property, or creating a debt or liability therefor, and no other ordinance, shall be passed at the same meeting at which it was introduced, unless by unanimous consent, or at a special meeting called therefor; and every such ordinance, resolution, or proceeding, shall be passed by yeas and nays, to be entered on the record; and, upon the demand of one-fourth of the members present, the yeas and nays shall be taken on any question and entered on the record. Money resolution, etc., not to be passed at same meeting at which it is introduced. Exception. Yeas and Nays.

Aldermen interested not to vote.

SEC. 18. No Alderman shall vote on any question in which he is interested; on all other questions every Alderman present shall vote, and in all cases of a tie vote, the question shall be lost.

Appointments and removals by a majority vote.

SEC. 19. All appointments to office shall be made by a majority vote of all the Aldermen elected, and removals from office shall be made by the like vote, except in cases where, by this act, a different vote may be required.

Standing Committees.

SEC. 20. The President of the Common Council shall appoint such committees as the Common Council may deem necessary. The duties of standing committees shall be prescribed by general ordinance.

Powers of Chairman of Committees.

SEC. 21. The chairman of any committee, and the members of any board, established by or under this act, may administer oaths and take affidavits in respect to any matter pending before such committee or board; such committees or board shall have power to subpœna witnesses, to compel their attendance, and the production of necessary papers in all examinations pending before them, and to that end the Common Council may prescribe and regulate the necessary proceedings, and confer upon the Marshal, or other officer of the corporation, all needful powers for the purposes aforesaid.

Powers of Council.

SEC. 22. The Common Council, in addition to its other powers under this act, and subject to and consistently with its provisions, shall have power within the limits and jurisdiction of the corporation:

Compensat'n of officers.

1st. To determine and regulate the compensation of all officers elected or appointed under this act, except as is herein otherwise provided; but the compensation of no officer, fixed by an annual or periodical salary, shall be diminished during the term for which he was elected or appointed. The salary of no officer shall be increased during his term of office, unless by a two-thirds vote of the Common Council.

Salary.

2d. To provide for and regulate the election and appointment of all officers, and for their removal from office, and for the filling of vacancies, subject to this act. Appointments and removals.

3d. To authorize and regulate the demand and receipt, by officers, of such fees and costs, and in such cases as the Common Council may deem reasonable. Fees and costs.

4th. To fix and regulate the fees of jurors and witnesses, in any proceeding under this act, or under any ordinance of the Common Council. Fees of jurors and witnesses.

5th. To provide for and preserve the purity and salubrity of the waters of the Detroit River; to prohibit and prevent the depositing therein of all filthy and other matter tending to render said water impure, unwholesome, or offensive; to preserve and regulate the navigation of the said river, within the limits of said city; to prohibit and prevent the depositing or keeping therein any structure, earth, or substance, tending to obstruct or impair the navigation thereof, and remove all obstructions that may, at any time, occur therein; and to direct and regulate the stationing, anchoring, and mooring of vessels, and laying out of cargoes and ballast from the same. River Detroit

6th. To license, continue, and regulate so many ferries from within said city, to the opposite shore of the Detroit River, for carrying and transporting persons and property across said river, in such manner as shall seem most conducive to the public good. Ferries.

7th. To erect, repair, and regulate public wharves and docks at the ends of streets, and on the property of the corporation; to regulate the erection and repair of private wharves and docks, so that they shall not extend into the Detroit River, beyond a certain line to be established by the Common Council; and to prohibit the encumbering of all public wharves and docks, with boxes, carriages, carts, drays, sleighs, sleds, or other vehicle or thing whatsoever. Wharves and docks.

8th. To lease the wharves and wharfing privileges at the ends of streets, on the Detroit River, in said city, upon such Leases of wharves.

terms and conditions, and under such covenants, and with such remedies, in case of non-performance, as the Common Council may direct; but no buildings shall be erected thereon. No lease thereof shall be executed for a longer period than three years, and a free passage at all times, for all persons, with their baggage, over said public wharves.

Highways and streets. 9th. To work and improve all highways, avenues, streets, lanes, alleys, and public spaces within said city; to assess and levy upon all taxable property within said city, and expend such highway taxes as may be necessary therefor, and to elect whether the same shall be collected in money or labor, in such amount as the Common Council shall prescribe for each ward respectively: Proviso. *Provided*, Such highway taxes shall not in amount exceed the rates now fixed by law, and the same shall be collected, assessed, and levied as other taxes.

Public parks, etc. 10th. To make, grade, improve, and adorn the public parks, squares, spaces, and all grounds in said city, belonging to or under the control of the corporation, and to control and regulate the same consistently with the purposes and objects thereof.

Opening streets, etc. 11th. To establish, open, widen, extend, straighten, alter, vacate, and abolish highways, streets, avenues, lanes, alleys, and public grounds, or spaces, within said city; and to grade, pave, repair, and otherwise improve the highways, streets, avenues, lanes, alleys, or interior public spaces, created by the intersection of streets, crosswalks, and sidewalks in said city, with stone, wood, brick, or other material; and the Common Council shall have full power and authority to Paving costs and expenses provide for paying the costs and expenses thereof, by assessment on the owner of the lot or premises in front of or adjacent to which such highways, streets, avenues, lanes, alleys, interior or public spaces, crosswalks or sidewalks, may be directed to be graded, paved, re-paved, or otherwise improved: Proviso. *Provided*, That the cost of such grading, paving, repairing, or improving such interior or public spaces shall be assessed to each block, in such proportion as the Common Council shall deem just and equitable: *Provided, further*, That each block shall only be assessed to the center of such interior or public spaces, each way; which assessment shall be a lien, until paid, on such lot or premises in front of or adjacent to which such grading, paving, repairing, and improving may be directed, and shall be collected in the same manner as other assessments or taxes imposed by authority of the Common Council. Whenever such grading, paving, repairing, and improving shall be at the intersection of two or more avenues or streets, and in front of or adjacent to the point of a triangular block, such portion of the costs and expenses thereof shall be assessed to and paid by the City of Detroit, as the Common Council shall deem just. 2d Proviso.

12th. To sell, or otherwise provide for disposing of all dirt, filth, manure and cleanings, lying in or gathered from highways, streets, avenues, lanes, alleys, and public spaces, and all earth to be removed therefrom, or from the public squares and grounds of said city, in grading, paving, or otherwise improving the same. Dirt, etc.

13th. To clean the highways, streets, avenues, lanes, alleys, public grounds and squares, crosswalks and sidewalks, in said city, of filth, mud, and other substances; to prohibit and prevent the incumbering thereof with boxes, signs, posts, and all other materials or things whatsoever, and to remove the same therefrom; to prevent the exhibition of signs on canvas, or otherwise, in and upon any vehicle, standing or traveling, upon the streets of said city; to control, prescribe, and regulate the mode of constructing and suspending awnings, and the exhibition and suspension of signs therein; to compel the occupants of lots to clear the sidewalks in front of and adjacent thereto, of snow, ice, dirt, mud, boxes, and every incumbrance or obstruction thereon; to control, prescribe, and regulate the manner in which the highways, streets, avenues, lanes, alleys, public grounds, and spaces, within said city, shall be used and enjoyed; to direct and Cleaning streets, etc.

regulate the planting, and provide for the preservation of ornamental trees therein; to provide for and regulate the lighting of the same, and the erection of lamps and lamp-posts therein; to prohibit and prevent racing, and fast or dangerous driving and riding therein; to prohibit and prevent the flying of kites, and all practices, amusements, and doings therein, having a tendency to frighten teams and horses, or dangerous to life or property; to remove, or cause to be removed, all walls and other structures that may be liable to fall therein, or otherwise, so as to endanger life or property.

Riots, etc.

14th. To prohibit and prevent any riot, rout, disorderly noise, disturbance, or assemblage, or the crying of any goods in the streets, or elsewhere in said city.

Quiet on docks and streets.

15th. To preserve quiet and order on the docks, and in the streets of said city, at the arrival and departure of rail road cars, steamboats, and other vessels, and prescribe and regulate the manner and places in which drivers, porters, runners, solicitors, agents, and baggage collectors for hotels, or public houses, or express companies, draymen, cabmen, cartmen, hackmen, omnibus drivers, and solicitors for passengers, or for baggage, with their drays, carts, cabs, carriages, sleighs, or other vehicles shall stand, and to prohibit or prevent them from entering or driving within any rail road depot, or upon any wharf or dock, or entering upon any steamboat, or other vessel, to solicit passengers, or for baggage.

Stands for vehicles.

16th. To prescribe places or stands in the streets of said city, within which drays, carts, cabs, hacks, coaches, carriages, sleighs, sleds, and other vehicles may stand and be kept for hire, and within which loads of wood, coal, hay, and other articles may be kept for sale, and to regulate such stands and places.

Fire-works.

17th. To prohibit and prevent the exhibition of fire-works, and firing of cannon, or any fire-arms, which the Common Council may deem dangerous to life or property.

18th. To permit any person to pave or plank the sidewalks in front of the premises owned or occupied by such person, in said city, under the direction of the Street Commissioners, or some other officer of the corporation, and according to such regulations as the Common Council shall prescribe; and whenever any street shall have been paved, graveled, planked, or macadamised by the Common Council, and the assessment for the costs and expenses thereof has been duly paid to the corporation, such person shall not be assessed or compelled to pay any district, road, or highway tax on the premises in front of which such pavement shall have been made, so long as he shall keep the same in repair, to the satisfaction of the Common Council. Paving sidewalks.

19th. To prohibit and prevent, in the streets or elsewhere in said city, indecent exposure of the person, the show, sale, or exhibition for sale, of indecent or obscene pictures, drawings, engravings, paintings, and books or pamphlets, and all indecent or obscene exhibitions, and shows of every kind. Indecent exposure of person, etc.

20th. To prohibit and prevent, or regulate the leading and driving, or running at large, of cattle, horses, asses, mules, swine, sheep, goats, geese, and domestic fowls, in the streets, or elsewhere in said city, and to impound the same, when running at large, in one or more sufficient pounds, to be provided and maintained by the city, and to sell the same to pay the costs of proceedings, and any penalty thereby incurred, rendering the surplus, if any, to the owner. Cattle at large in streets.

21st. To prohibit and prevent, or regulate the running at large of dogs, to require them to be muzzled, and to authorize their destruction, when running at large in violation of any ordinance of the Common Council; to compel persons to fasten or secure their horses, oxen, or other animals, attached to vehicles, or otherwise, while standing or remaining in the streets, lanes, or alleys of said city; to prohibit and prevent persons from driving in vehicles, or otherwise, upon or across the sidewalks of said city. Dogs. Securing teams. Driving on side-walks.

Bridges, culverts, sewers and drains.

22d. To establish, construct, maintain, repair, enlarge, and discontinue, within the highways, streets, avenues, lanes, alleys, and public spaces of said city, such bridges, culverts, sewers, drains, and lateral drains and sewers, as the Common Council may see fit, with a view to the proper sewerage and drainage of said city; to compel the owners of all occupied lots, premises, and subdivisions thereof, within said city, to construct private drains or sewers therefrom, to connect with some public sewer or drain. Said private drains and sewers shall be constructed in such manner, and of such form and dimensions, and under such regulations, as the Common Council shall prescribe.

Assessment on cellars, lots, etc.

23d. To assess, levy, and collect an annual assessment, or tax, on all lots and subdivisions thereof, and on all cellars, drained by private drains or sewers, connected with any public sewer or drain, as hereafter further provided.

Boundaries of city and streets.

24th. To survey, ascertain, and establish the boundaries of the city, and of all highways, streets, avenues, lanes, alleys, public parks, squares, and spaces in said city; to prohibit and remove all encroachments upon the same, by buildings, fences, or in any other manner; and to number the buildings, the expense of such numbering to be assessed against and collected of the owner or occupant.

Number buildings.

Draining swamps.

25th. To provide for the draining of any swamp, marsh, wet or low lands, in said city, or within the distance of three miles therefrom, by the opening of ditches; but a jury, of not less than six disinterested freeholders, of the County of Wayne, before any proposed ditch can be opened, shall ascertain that the opening thereof is necessary or proper; also, whether the benefits which will accrue to the owner or owners of any lands, from the opening of the ditch, will or will not be equal to any damages he or they will sustain thereby. If such benefits are exceeded by the damages, they shall ascertain and certify the damages to which the owner or owners will be entitled, after deducting therefrom the amount of benefits their lands will receive, from the opening of the proposed ditch. On payment, or tender of the damages thus ascertained and certified, the Common Council shall have power to enter upon any land through which the proposed ditch will run, with the necessary agents, teams, and implements, to cut and open said ditch, to protect, clean, and scour it from time to time, so as to preserve its original dimensions, and to prohibit and prevent all obstruction thereof, or injury thereto.

26th. To erect and maintain market houses, establish markets and market places; to lease market stalls, booths, and stands; to provide fully for the good government and regulations thereof, and to prohibit, prevent, and punish forestalling and regrating. Markets.

27th. To provide for the preservation of the general health of the inhabitants of said city; to make regulations to secure the same; to prevent the introduction or spreading of contagious or infectious diseases; to prevent and suppress diseases generally, and, if deemed necessary, to establish a Board of Health, and prescribe and regulate its powers and duties. Public health

28th. To prohibit, prevent, abate, and remove all nuisances in said city, or within the distance therefrom of half a mile, and to punish the authors or maintainers thereof, and authorize and direct the speedy or immediate abatement or removal of nuisances, by some officer of said city. If, in order to abate or remove any nuisance, the Common Council shall deem it necessary to fill up, level, or drain any lot or premises, they shall have power so to do; to assess the cost and expenses of such filling, leveling, or draining, and impose the same as an assessment or tax on said lot or premises, which shall be a lien thereon, till paid, and shall be collected in the same manner as other taxes and assessments, levied and imposed by authority of the Common Council. Abatement of nuisances.

29th. To compel the owner or occupant of any grocery, cellar, tallow-chandler's shop, soap, candle, starch, or glue factory, tannery, butcher's shop, or stall, slaughter house, Nuisances.

stable, barn, privy, sewer, or other unwholesome or nauseous house, or place, to cleanse, or abate the same, whenever necessary for the health, comfort, or convenience of the inhabitants of said city.

Nuisances. 30th. To prohibit and prevent any person from burying, depositing, or leaving within the limits of said city, or within one mile distant therefrom, or keeping, or having, on the premises owned or occupied by him, in said city, any dead carcass, putrid or unsound beef, pork, fish, hides and skins, and any article, substance, or thing that is unwholesome, or nauseous, and to compel and authorize the removal thereof by some officer of said city; or to compel any person so bringing, depositing, or leaving the same within the limits of said city, or one mile distant therefrom, or having or keeping the same on the premises owned or occupied by him, in said city, to remove the same.

Cellars. 31st. To direct and regulate the construction of cellars, slips, barns, private drains, sinks, and privies; to compel the owner or occupant to fill up, drain, cleanse, alter, relay, or repair the same, or to cause the same to be done by some officer of the corporation, and assess the expenses thereof on the lot or premises having such cellar, slip, barn, private drain, sink, or privy thereon, which assessment shall be a lien on such lot or premises, and be collected in the same manner as other assessments, imposed by authority of the Common Council. To direct and regulate the construction of lateral sewers, or drains, for the purpose of more effectually draining all lots, or cellars, yards, and sinks, within the limits of said city, whenever, in their opinion, the same shall be necessary: *Provided*, Such lateral sewers or drains shall be laid or constructed through any of the streets and alleys adjoining, or in front of the premises through which sewers or drains shall be ordered constructed, and assess the expense thereof on such lots or premises benefitted thereby, which assessment shall be a lien on such lots or premises, until paid, and be collected in the same manner as other assessments, imposed by authority of the Common Council.

Proviso.

32d. To establish a fire department; to provide for the prevention and extinguishment of fires, and to establish, organize, and regulate fire companies, in the manner elsewhere prescribed in this act. Fire Department.

33d. To prohibit and prevent, within certain limits in said city, to be determined by the Common Council, the location or construction of buildings for storing powder, powder factories, tanneries, distilleries, buildings for the manufacture of turpentine, camphene, and dangerous or easily inflammable, or explosive substances, slaughter houses and yards, butchering shops, soap, candle, starch, and glue factories, establishments for steaming or rendering lard, tallow, offal, and such other substances as can be rendered into tallow, lard, or oil, and all establishments where any nauseous, offensive, or unwholesome business may be carried on. And such buildings, factories, shops, and establishments as aforesaid, now or hereafter to be constructed, in said city, whether within or without the limits, to be determined as aforesaid, together with blacksmith shops, foundries, cooper shops, steam boiler factories, carpenter shops, planing establishments, breweries, and all buildings and establishments usually regarded as extra-hazardous in respect to fire, shall be subject to such regulations in relation to their construction and management, as the Common Council may make, with a view to the protection of any property from injury by fire, or to the health and safety of the inhabitants of said city, and to prevent their becoming in any way nuisances. Powder or other factory or buildings.

34th. To regulate the keeping and conveyance, in said city, of powder and other combustible or dangerous articles, and the use and kind of lights or lamps to be used in barns, stables, and all buildings and establishments usually regarded as extra-hazardous, in respect to fire. Safe-guards against fire.

35th. To prohibit and prevent the location or construction of any wooden or frame house, store, shop, or other building, on such streets, alleys, and places, or within such Wooden buildings, construction, removal and re-building.

limits in said city as the Common Council may, from time to time, prescribe; to prohibit and prevent the removing of wooden or frame buildings from any part of said city, to any lot on such streets, alleys, and places, or within said limits, and the rebuilding and repairing of the same; to prevent the rebuilding or repairing of wooden buildings on said streets, alleys, and places, or within said limits, when damaged by fire, or otherwise.

May be prohibited.

Partition fences, walls, chimneys, etc.

36th. To regulate the construction of partition fences, and of partition and parapet walls, the thickness of walls, and the size of brick; to regulate the construction of chimneys, hearths, fire-places, fire-arches, ovens, and the putting up of stoves, stove-pipes, kettles, boilers, or any structure or apparatus that may be dangerous in causing or promoting fires; to prohibit and prevent the burning out of chimneys and chimney flues; to compel and regulate the cleaning thereof, and fix the fees therefor; to compel and regulate the construction of ash-houses, or deposits for ashes; to compel the owners of houses, and other buildings, to have scuttles upon the roofs thereof, and stairs or ladders leading to the same; to appoint one or more officers to enter into all buildings and inclosures, to discover whether the same are in a dangerous state, and to cause such as are in a dangerous state, to be put in a safe condition; to authorize any of the officers of the city to keep away from the vicinity of a fire, all idle or suspicious persons, and to compel all officers of the city, and other persons, to aid in the extinguishment of fires, and in the preservation of property exposed to danger therefrom.

Safe-guards against fire.

Officers at fires.

Bathing.

37th. To prohibit and prevent, or to regulate bathing and swimming in any of the waters in and adjoining said city, determine the times and places thereof, and prohibit and prevent any obscene or indecent exhibition, exposure, or conduct thereat.

Houses of ill-fame and assignation.

38th. To prohibit, prevent, and suppress the keeping of houses of ill-fame, or assignation, or for the resort of common prostitutes, disorderly houses, and disorderly groceries; to restrain, suppress, and punish the keepers thereof; to punish, restrain, and prevent common prostitutes, vagrants, mendicants, street beggars, drunken or disorderly persons; to prohibit, prevent, and suppress mock auctions, and every kind of fraudulent game, devise, or practice, and punish all persons managing, using, practicing, or attempting to manage, use, or practice the same, and all persons aiding in the management, use, or practice thereof. Games.

39th. To prohibit, prevent, and suppress the sale of every kind of unsound, nauseous, and unwholesome meat, poultry, fish, vegetables, or other articles of food and provisions, and impure or spurious wines and spiritous liquors, and to punish all persons who shall knowingly sell the same, or offer or keep the same for sale. Unsound meats.

40th. To prohibit, restrain, and prevent persons from gaming for money, with cards, dice, billiards, nine or ten pin alleys, tables, ball alleys, wheels of fortune, boxes, machines, or other instruments or devices whatsoever, in any grocery, store, shop, or any other place in said city; to punish the persons keeping the building, instruments, or means for such gaming, and compel the destruction of the same. Gaming.

41st. To prohibit, prevent, and suppress all lotteries for the drawing or disposing of money, or any other property, whatsoever, and to punish all persons maintaining, directing, or managing the same, or aiding in the maintenance, direction, or management thereof. Lotteries.

42d. To prohibit and prevent persons from selling or giving away ardent spirits, or other intoxicating liquors, to any child, apprentice, or servant, without the consent of his or her parent, guardian, master, or mistress; to license and regulate the selling or giving away of any ardent spirits, or other intoxicating liquors, by any shop-keeper, trader, grocer, inn, hotel, or tavern keeper, keeper of any ordinary, saloon, recess, victualing, or other house, or by any other Intoxicating liquors.

person, in case the selling or giving away of ardent spirits, and other intoxicating liquors, and licensing the sale thereof, shall hereafter be authorized by the laws of the State.

To license porters and runners.

43d. To license and regulate solicitors of passengers or for baggage for the benefit of any hotel, tavern, public house, boat or railroad, also draymen, carmen, truckmen, porters, runners, drivers of cabs, hackney coaches, omnibusses, carriages, sleighs, express vehicles and vehicles of every other description used and employed for hire, and to fix and regulate the amount and rates of their compensation.

Auctioneers, peddlers, etc.

44th. To license and regulate auctioneers, hawkers, peddlers and pawn-brokers, and regulate auctions, hawking, peddling and pawn-brokerage; to license and regulate the peddling and hawking of fruits, nuts, cakes, refreshments, jewelry, merchandise, goods and other property whatsoever, by hand, hand-cart, show-case, show-stand or otherwise in the public streets.

Public exhibitions.

45th. To prohibit and prevent, or license and regulate the public exhibition by itinerant persons, or companies, of natural or artificial curiosities, caravans, circuses, menageries, theatrical representations, concerts, musical entertainments, exhibitions of common showmen, and shows of any kind.

Hotels, etc.

46th. To license and regulate the keepers of hotels, taverns and other public houses, grocers and keepers of ordinaries, saloons, and victualling, or other houses or places for furnishing meals, food or drink.

Butchers, provision dealers, etc.

47th. To license and regulate butchers; to license and regulate or suppress hucksters, and to license and regulate the keepers of shops, stalls, booths or stands at markets or any other place in said city, for the sale of any kind of meat, fish, poultry, vegetables, food or provisions.

Billiards and pin alleys.

48th. To license and regulate keepers of billiard tables, pin alleys, nine or ten pin alleys, but not for the purpose of gaming.

49th. To license and regulate public bath houses or bath rooms on land, and any public floating bath houses, bath rooms or vessels on the Detroit River. Bath houses.

50th. To establish and regulate an efficient system of police for the good government of said city; to appoint, on the recommendation of the Mayor or acting Mayor, policemen and watchmen, who shall possess and exercise the same powers, as conservators of the peace, which township Constables, under the general laws of this State, possess, and to prescribe and regulate their further powers and duties, and fix their compensation. Said policemen and watchmen may be removed at any time by the Common Council, on the recommendation of the Mayor or acting Mayor. Police. Removal of policemen.

51st. To appoint one or more inspectors, measurers, weighers and guagers of articles to be measured, inspected, weighed and guaged; to prescribe and regulate their powers and duties, fees and compensation. Weighers and guagers.

52d. To direct and regulate the weight and quantity of bread, the size of the loaf, and the inspecting thereof. Bread.

53d. To direct and regulate the inspecting and measuring of wood, lumber, shingles, timber, posts, stones, heading and all building materials; the inspecting, measuring and weighing of coke and all kinds of coal; the inspecting and weighing of hay; the inspecting of vegetables, fresh, dried, smoked, salted, pickled, and other meat, or fish, poultry, butter, lard, and other food or provisions to be sold at wholesale or retail; the inspecting and weighing of flour, meal, pork, beef, and all other food or provisions, and salt, to be sold in half-barrels, barrels, casks, hogsheads, boxes, or other packages; and the inspecting and guaging of oils, wines, whisky, and other spiritous liquors, to be sold at wholesale or retail, or in kegs, half-barrels, barrels, casks, hogsheads, or other vessels: *Provided*, That nothing herein contained shall be construed to authorize the inspecting, measuring, weighing, or guaging of any article herein enumerated, which is to be shipped beyond the limits of this State, except at the Inspection of wood, etc. Proviso.

request of the owner thereof or of the agent having charge of the same.

Weights and measures. 54th. To regulate the weights and measures to be used in said city, and compel every merchant, retailer, trader and dealer in merchandise, groceries, provisions or property of any description which is sold by measure or weight, to use weights and measures to be sealed by the city sealer, and to be subject to his inspection and alteration, so as to be made conformable to the standard of weights and measures established by the general laws of the State.

Paupers. 55th. To provide for the protection and care of paupers, and to prohibit and prevent all persons from bringing, in vessels or in any other mode, to said city, from any other port or place, any pauper or other person likely to become a charge upon said city, and to punish therefor.

Burial of paupers, etc. 56th. To provide for the burial of strangers and poor deceased persons; to regulate the burial of the dead and the registrations of births and deaths, and to order and compel the keeping and returning of bills of mortality by physicians, sextons and others.

Births, deaths, etc.

Census. 57th. To provide for taking a census of the inhabitants of said city, whenever the Common Council may see fit, and to direct and regulate the same; to provide for calling meetings of the inhabitants of said city by public notice thereof, fixing the time and place of meeting, and to regulate the ringing of bells.

Public meetings.

Public buildings. 58th. To erect and provide for the erection of a City Hall and all needful buildings and offices for the use of the corporation or of its officers, and to control and regulate the same.

Alms House Department. 59th. To establish, organize and maintain an Alms-House Department, to purchase the necessary grounds, and erect and provide for erecting the necessary buildings therefor, either within or without the city limits.

Jails, work houses and houses of correction. 60th. To establish and build jails, work houses and houses of correction for the confinement of offenders; to erect and provide for erecting the necessary buildings therefor, and control and regulate the same; to appoint all necessary officers for taking charge of the same and of persons confined therein; to prescribe their powers and duties, and provide for their removal from office and the filling of vacancies.

61st. To imprison and confine in said jails, work houses and houses of correction, at hard labor or otherwise, all persons liable to be imprisoned or confined under this act or any ordinance of the Common Council, or lawfully committed thereto by any court or magistrate, as herein provided. Any court or magistrate in the City of Detroit or the County of Wayne may commit to any work house or house of correction of said city, instead of the jail of Wayne County, any person convicted of an offense against the general laws of the State, now or hereafter punishable by imprisonment in the jail of Wayne County. Any court of competent jurisdiction of the State of Michigan may, in its discretion, commit any male under sixteen, or female under fourteen years of age, to any work house or house of correction of said city, instead of the State prison, who shall be convicted of any crime now or hereafter punishable by imprisonment in the State prison, whenever in the opinion of the court the welfare of the public and of the convict will be promoted thereby. All expenses attending the confinement of any person sentenced to be committed to any work house or house of correction of said city for any offense against the general laws of this State, now or hereafter punishable by imprisonment in the State prison, shall be paid by the State Treasurer quarter-yearly, on the certificate of the City Controller that such expenses have been incurred. All expenses attending the confinement of any person sentenced to be committed to any work house or house of correction of said city for any offense against the general laws of the State, now or hereafter not punishable by imprisonment in the State prison, shall be paid quarter-yearly by the Treasurer of the County in which the offender was tried and convicted, upon the certificate of the City Controller that such expenses have been incurred. Imprisonment.

Speed of cars — 62d. To prescribe and regulate the speed of cars and engines on railroads within the limits of said city.

Licenses by Mayor. — 63d. To authorize the Mayor to grant, issue and revoke licenses in all cases where licenses may be granted and issued under this act and the ordinances of the Common Council; to direct the manner of issuing and registring the same, and to prescribe the sum of money to be paid therefor into the treasury of the corporation. No license shall be granted for more than one year, and the person receiving the same shall, before the issuing thereof, execute a bond to the corporation in such sum as the Common Council may prescribe, with one or more sufficient sureties, conditioned for a faithful observance of the charter of the corporation and the ordinances of the Common Council, and otherwise conditioned as the Common Council may prescribe. The Mayor may inquire into the sufficiency of the sureties in such bond by an examination under oath as to their property and responsibility, which oath may be administered by him. The depositions of the sureties shall be reduced to writing, be signed by him, certified by the Mayor, annexed to and filed with the bond to which it relates, in the office of the Clerk of the City.

Taxes. — 64th. To assess, levy, and collect taxes for the purposes of the corporation upon all property made taxable by law for State purposes, which taxes shall be liens upon the property taxed till paid; to make regulations for assessing, levying and collecting the same, and to sell the property taxed to pay the taxes thereon.

Appropriat'n of money. — 65th. To appropriate money, provide for the payment of the debt and expenses of the said city, and make regulations concerning the same.

Punishment of offenders. — 66th. To punish all offenders for violations of, or offenses against this act, or any ordinance of the Common Council enacted under this or any other act of the Legislature, by holding to bail for good behavior, by imposing fines, penalties, forfeitures and costs, and by imprisonment in the jail of Wayne County, any jail, work house, house of correction, or alms house of said city, or by either, in the discretion of the court or magistrate before whom conviction may be had. If only a fine, penalty or forfeiture be imposed, together with the costs, the offender may be sentenced to be imprisoned until the payment thereof, for a term not exceeding six months. All punishments for offenses against the ordinances of the Common Council shall be prescribed in the ordinance creating or specifying the offense to be punished; and no penalty or forfeiture shall exceed one thousand dollars, no fine shall exceed five hundred dollars, and no imprisonment shall exceed the period of two years.

67th. To employ all persons confined for the non-payment of any fine, penalty, forfeiture or costs, or for any offense under this act or any ordinance of the Common Council, in the jail of Wayne County, or any jail, work house, house of correction, or alms house of said city, at work or labor, either, within or without the same, or upon the streets of said city, or any public work under the control of the Common Council; to allow any person thus confined for the non-payment of any fine, penalty, forfeiture or costs, to pay and discharge the same by such work or labor, and to fix the value and rates of such work and labor. Employment of prisoners.

68th. To provide for printing and publishing all matters required to be printed and published under this act or by order of the Common Council, in such manner as said Common Council may prescribe. Printing.

69th. To provide for maintaining the peace, order and good government of the City of Detroit. The Common Council shall have power to subdivide the City of Detroit into wards. Public peace. Wards.

70th. The Common Council shall have power to purchase and sell real estate for the use of said corporation, for corporate purposes, and to execute mortgages on the same, for any balance which may remain unpaid on the purchase money paid for such real estate. They shall also have power to purchase and control land for cemetery purposes, either within or without the corporation limits of said city. Purchase real estate.

The Common Council shall also have power :

To regulate construction of buildings.

1st. To regulate the construction of stone or brick buildings, the thickness of walls, and the size of brick.

To perpetuate evidence of title.

2d. To adopt such measures as may be deemed expedient to perpetuate evidence of title of real estate, by the preservation of maps, plats, records, and papers relating thereto.

To appoint policemen and watchmen.

Powers of policemen.

3d. To appoint, on the nomination of Police Commissioners, Policemen and Watchmen, who shall hold their office during the pleasure of the Common Council, unless sooner removed by said Board, as aforesaid. The Policemen so appointed, shall have power to serve any summons, subpœna, warrant, order, notice, paper, or process whatever, issued or directed by any Justice of the Peace, Judge, Court, or officer whatever, in the execution of the laws of the State, for the prevention of crimes, and the punishment of criminal offenders, or of the police laws, and regulations of the State or city, in any proceeding collateral to, or connected with the execution of such general laws, and police laws and regulations. They shall have power to serve any process for any violations of the city ordinances, and generally shall have and exercise the powers, as conservators of the peace, which Township Constables, under the general laws of the State possess; but such Policemen shall have no power to serve any paper or process in any civil action, or any paper connected therewith. The Mayor, or acting Mayor, shall make no nomination of Policemen, or Watchmen, unless thereto requested by the Police Commissioners. [*As amended by Section* 19 *of the Act of* 1861.

# CHAPTER VI.

## RECORDER'S COURT.



SECTION 1. There shall be a Municipal Court in and for the City of Detroit, to be called "The Recorder's Court," which shall be a court of record. *Recorder's Court, Court of Record.*

SEC. 2. The Recorder of said city shall be the Judge of said Court, but in case of his absence from the city, inability to attend, or a vacancy in his office, one of the Judges of the Circuit Court, to be previously designated by the Recorder, or the Common Council, shall be the Judge of said Court, and, as such Judge, have and exercise all the powers and duties of said Recorder, until he shall resume his office, or such vacancy be filled. *Recorder to be Judge, etc.*

Clerk of Court, his duty and powers.

SEC. 3. There shall be a Clerk of said Court, as before provided in this act, whose duty it shall be to keep a true record of the proceedings of said court, in proper books to be provided therefor, and file and safely keep all books and papers belonging or pertaining to said court. He shall sign and seal all writs and process issuing from said court, and shall have power generally, to administer oaths and take affidavits.

Sheriff and deputy to attend Recorder's Court.

SEC. 4. The Sheriff of Wayne County, and his deputies, shall attend the sittings of said court, and it shall be their duty, and they shall have power to execute, under the direction of the Sheriff, all lawful precepts and commands of said court, and serve and execute all lawful writs and process issuing therefrom.

Jurisdiction of Recorder's Court.

SEC. 5. The said Recorder's Court shall have original and exclusive jurisdiction of all prosecutions and proceedings in behalf of the people of this State, for crimes, misdemeanors, and offenses arising under the laws of this State, and committed within the corporate limits of the City of Detroit, except in cases cognizable by the Police Court of the city of Detroit, or by the Justices of the Peace of the said city; and shall have power to issue all lawful writs and process, and to do all lawful acts which may be necessary and proper, to carry into complete effect the powers and jurisdiction given by this act, and especially to issue all writs and process, and to do all acts which the Circuit Courts of this State, within their respective jurisdictions, may, in like cases, issue and do, by the laws of this State: *Provided*, That this section shall not be construed to prevent the grand jury for the County of Wayne from inquiring into and presenting indictments, as heretofore, for crimes and offenses committed within the limits of said city: *Provided, further*, That this act shall not in any way affect the jurisdiction of the Circuit Court for the County of Wayne, over any case now pending in said court, nor the validity of any recognizance, as heretofore made to said court.

Proviso.

2d Proviso.

SEC. 6. Prosecutions in the Recorder's Court, for crimes, misdemeanors, and offenses, arising under the laws of this State, and within the jurisdiction of said court, may be either by information, complaint, or indictment. Prosecuti'ns, how commenced.

SEC. 7. Such informations and complaints shall be in the name of the People of the State of Michigan, shall be signed by the Prosecuting Attorney, shall be certified by the oath of the prosecuting, or of some complaining witness, and shall have thereon indorsed the names of witnesses, as is required in cases of indictments, and shall have, in the statement of the offense or offenses charged, the same preciseness and fullness in matters of substance, as is required in indictments in like cases, in the courts of this State, and the same may be amended in like manner as is provided in cases of indictment. Different offenses, or different degrees of the same offense, may be joined in one information, or complaint, in all cases where the same might be joined by different counts in one indictment; and in all cases, a defendant, or defendants, shall have the same rights in all subsequent pleadings and proceedings, as he or they would have, if prosecuted for the same offense by indictment. Form of information and complaints. Contents. Joinder of offenses. Rights of defendants.

SEC. 8. No information or complaint shall be filed against any person, for either of the crimes of treason, murder, arson, rape, or perjury, unless the same shall first be laid before the judge of said court, and he shall thereon indorse a direction that the same be filed. Information or complait's in certain cases.

SEC. 9. Where an offense consists of different degrees, the defendant, or defendants may be found guilty of any degree of the offense, inferior to the one charged in the information or complaint, or of any attempt to commit the same. Degrees of offenses.

SEC. 10. All provisions of law, relative to the joinder of persons or offenders, in one indictment, and relative to subsequent pleadings and proceedings in cases of indictment, in either the court of original or appellate jurisdiction, or in General laws of State to apply.

the execution of any sentence, shall be applicable, so far as may be, to prosecutions by information or complaint, under this act, for offenses against the laws of this State.

Jurisdiction of recognizance. SEC. 11. Said Recorder's Court shall have full jurisdiction and authority to control and enforce all recognizances, lawfully taken by said court, or by the Judge thereof, or by any other court, judge, or magistrate, in the course of any prosecution or proceeding pending in said court, or lawfully taken by any court, judge, or magistrate, to compel any person or persons to appear before said Recorder's Court, and there to answer and do according to the terms thereof, and whenever default shall be made in any such recognizances, such default shall be duly entered of record in said Recorder's Court, and thereafter said court shall, upon the motion of the Prosecuting Attorney, summarily enter judgment against all the parties liable on said recognizance, for the full amount thereof: *Provided, however*, That any person against whom such judgment may have been entered, shall have the right to apply to the court within twenty days after the rendition of such judgment, for the vacation of the same, for good cause shown, and said court may thereupon, in its discretion, vacate such judgment on such terms as it may deem just. Execution shall be awarded and executed upon said judgment in like manner as is provided in personal actions.

Proviso.

Form of recognizance. SEC. 12. All such recognizances as are mentioned in the preceding section, may be in the usual form, or may contain a further clause, authorizing said Recorder's Court, upon default in said recognizances, summarily to enter judgment upon the same, against the several parties liable thereon, for the full amount of such recognizance.

Indictments presented to Circuit Court for Wayne county to be certified to Recorder's Court. SEC. 13. All indictments for offenses committed within the limits of the city of Detroit, which may be found and presented to the Circuit Court for the County of Wayne, by the grand jury of said county, shall be forthwith certified and transmitted by the Clerk of said Circuit Court, to said Recorder's Court, and thereupon said Recorder's Court shall have a full and complete jurisdiction of said indictments, as if the same had been originally presented to said Recorder's Court, and shall have full power to take all further proceedings thereon.

SEC. 14. The Prosecuting Attorney for the County of Wayne, shall appear and act for the people of the State of Michigan, in said Recorder's Court, in all cases arising under the laws of this State, and he shall render to said court, in writing, and on oath, at the last term thereof in each year, an annual account of all moneys collected or received by him as the prosecuting officer of said court.

Prosecuting Attorney for Wayne county to act for the people in Recorder's Court.

To render account.

SEC. 15. The Judge of said Recorder's Court shall possess the same power to grant writs of habeas corpus, returnable before himself, and to adjudicate thereon, and do all acts in vacation touching any suit or proceeding in said court, as is now, or may be possessed by the Circuit Courts of the State, in matters before said Circuit Courts.

Recorder's powers in case of habeas corpus.

SEC. 16. The Judge of the Recorder's Court shall have all such powers and authority at chambers, touching any suit or proceeding in said Recorder's Court, as the Judges of the Circuit Courts now have, or may have, in like suits or proceedings before said Circuit Courts.

Powers of Judge at Chambers.

SEC. 17. The said Recorder's Court shall have power to make rules for regulating the practice, and conducting the business thereof, and to alter, amend, or repeal the same, in its discretion.

Rules of court, how made.

SEC. 18. Said Recorder's Court shall devise its own seal, at the expense of said city, and a description thereof, attested by the Clerk of said court, shall be deposited in the office of the Controller.

Seal.

SEC. 19. All writs and process, issuing from said Recorder's Court, on complaints under the city ordinances, shall be directed to the Marshal, or any Constable of said city, and may be served and executed by the officers to whom the same are directed, at any place within the limits of this State; and all writs and process for offenses under the general laws of the State, shall be directed to the Sheriff, shall

Writs, to whom directed and by whom and when served, form of, etc.

run "In the name of the People of the State of Michigan," be sealed with the seal of the court, signed by the Clerk of said court, dated on the day on which the same may issue, and tested in the name of the Recorder of said city.

Prosecuti'ns, how commenced.

SEC. 20. All prosecutions for offenses in said Recorder's Court, arising under this act, or under any ordinance or regulation of the Common Council, shall be in the name of the People of the State of Michigan, and be commenced by filing with the Clerk of said court a complaint, in writing, in the form of an affidavit, duly sworn to before said Clerk, and subscribed by the person making the complaint, and having indorsed thereon the proper jurat of said Clerk; and it shall be deemed sufficient to set forth, in said complaint, the offense complained of according to its substance. The trial shall be had and determined upon said complaint, and upon pleadings, which may be amended, in the same manner as indictments and pleadings under the general laws of the State.

Trial.

Proceedings in case of vacancy in office of Attorney.

SEC. 21. In case of a vacancy in the office of Attorney, his absence or inability to attend, said Recorder's Court may designate a suitable person to discharge the duties of said Attorney, until such vacancy be filled, according to the provisions of this act, or he shall resume his office; and the person thus designated, shall receive for his services a reasonable compensation, to be paid by the County of Wayne, and fixed and determined by the Board of Auditors of said county.

Recorder's Court, terms of.

SEC. 22. There shall be a term of said Recorder's Court once in each month, which shall commence on the first Monday thereof, and may be continued or adjourned from time to time, as long as said court may deem necessary for the transaction of its business; and if from any cause the Judge of said court shali be unable to hold the same on the first day of a term, the Clerk thereof shall have power to open said court, and adjourn it from day to day, until the Judge shall be able to attend, and in such case all prosecu-

Adjournm'nt of, etc.

tions, proceedings and matters pending in said court, shall stand continued, until such Judge can hold said court.

SEC. 23. Said Recorder's Court shall also have exclusive cognizance of all offenses against any ordinances of the Common Council of the City of Detroit. Exclusive cognizance of.

SEC. 24. All the proceedings of said Recorder's Court, at any time before or after final judgment or sentence, may be removed to the Supreme Court by writ of error or other process, in the same manner that like proceedings may, by law, be removed to the Supreme Court from the Circuit Courts of the State, and the Supreme Court shall proceed to adjudicate thereon in the same manner as on proceedings removed from said Circuit Courts. Writ of error to Supreme Court.

SEC. 25. It shall be the duty of the City Attorney to collect all fines and penalties imposed for offenses under this act or any ordinance or regulation of the Common Council of said city, which shall be reported in writing by the Clerk of said court, at the close of each term thereof, to said Common Council, and immediately after their collection or receipt by the City Attorney, shall be paid by him to the Treasurer of said city. City Attorn'y to collect fines and penalties.

SEC. 26. The Common Council of said city and the Board of Auditors of Wayne County, or any committee thereof appointed for the purpose, may at all reasonable times inspect the records and papers of said Recorder's Court, and the Clerk thereof shall give them, when requested, any information within his power or knowledge concerning such records and papers, and concerning all fines and penalties imposed by said court. Records open for inspection.

SEC. 27. The City of Detroit shall be liable for all reasonable costs and expenses, and board of prisoners incurred in prosecutions for offenses and proceedings in said Recorder's Court, arising under this act, or any ordinance or regulation of the Common Council of said city; and the County of Wayne shall be liable for all reasonable costs and expenses, and board of prisoners incurred in prosecutions for offenses City liable for expense of board of prisoners in certain cases. County liable for expenses in other cases.

and proceedings in said court, arising under the general laws of the State; but if there be a conviction and sentence of confinement in any work house, or house of correction of said city, for any offense now or hereafter punishable by imprisonment in the State prison, the expenses attending the confinement of the prisoner after sentence shall be paid by the State Treasurer quarter-yearly, on the certificate of the City Controller that such expenses have been incurred.

Salary of Recorder; of clerk.

SEC. 28. The salary to be paid to the Recorder shall be the same as is allowed, or may be from time to time allowed, to the Circuit Judges of the State, and shall be paid by the State, in the same manner as the Circuit Judges are paid. The Clerk of the Recorder's Court shall be paid by the City of Detroit, such salary as the Common Council may prescribe.

Prisoners may be imprisoned in county jail.

SEC. 29. Any person liable to be imprisoned or confined under this act or any ordinance or regulation of the Common Council of said city, may be so imprisoned or confined in the jail of Wayne County, and it shall be the duty of the keeper of said jail to receive and safely keep therein all persons thus subject to imprisonment or confinement, until legally discharged therefrom.

General laws to apply.

SEC. 30. Any law of this State for the safe keeping of prisoners in a county jail, or for preventing or punishing their escape or the aiding of them to escape, or any other act detrimental to their safe keeping in a county jail, shall apply to any jail, work house, or house of correction, established and provided under this act by the City of Detroit for the imprisonment or confinement of offenders, in the same manner and to the same effect as to a county jail.

Certain punishments to be prescribed by Common Council.

SEC. 31. Punishments not herein prescribed for offenses against this act, and for offenses against the ordinances and regulations of the Common Council, shall be prescribed by said Common Council.

Challenges of jurors.

SEC. 32. In all jury trials in said Recorder's Court, the person or persons on trial shall have the same right of challenge and other rights and benefits extended by law to persons on trial, by a jury in criminal cases before the Circuit Courts of the State, subject to the provisions of this act.

Trial by jury.

SEC. 33. In all trials upon indictments, the person or persons on trial shall be tried by a jury, unless the right to a trial by jury be, with consent of the court, waived. In all trials for offenses against this act or any ordinance or regulation of the Common Council of said city, the person or persons on trial shall be tried by the court, unless he or they shall request to be tried by a jury. Juries shall be obtained, summoned, drawn and sworn as hereinafter provided.

Smith vs. The People, Supreme Court, April term, 1861.

Selection of persons to serve as jurors.

SEC. 34. The Assessor of said city, at the time herein appointed to review the assessment rolls in each year, shall select from them, when completed, a list of three hundred persons to serve as jurors in all cases where juries may be required under this act or any ordinance or regulation of the Common Council; and the persons thus selected shall be qualified electors of the City of Detroit, shall be of fair character and sound judgment and understanding, and, so far as practicable, such as were not actually drawn, or did not serve as jurors during the preceding year. Said list shall be signed by said Assessor, returned to the Clerk of said Recorder's Court and filed in his office. If said Assessor shall refuse or, neglect to return the list of jurors, as above provided, the Judge of the Recorder's Court shall have power to compel him to make such return. For every day that said Assessor shall neglect or refuse to make such returns, after the time prescribed in this section, he shall forfeit the sum of one hundred dollars.

Penalty on Assessor for neglect to return a list of jurors.

Clerk's duties on receiving list.

SEC. 35. The Clerk of said court, on receiving said list, shall file it in his office, shall write the names of the persons thus selected on separate strips of paper of the same size and appearance, as nearly as may be, shall fold up each of said strips of paper in the same manner, so as to conceal the name thereon, and deposit and preserve the same in a box, to be called and labelled "jury box," and the persons whose names are thus returned and deposited in said jury box, shall be liable to serve as jurors for one year, and until another list shall be selected, returned and filed with said Clerk, and the names thereon deposited in said jury box in the manner aforesaid.

Old ballots to be destroyed.

SEC. 36. Before depositing in said jury box the names contained in any new list, the ballots deposited therein for the preceding year shall be taken out and destroyed, and it shall be the duty of the Judge of said court to attend and be present with the Clerk, when the ballots, containing the names of persons to serve as jurors, are deposited in said jury box or taken out to be destroyed.

New ballots to be put in jury box.

Drawing petit jurors.

SEC. 37. At least ten days before any term of said Recorder's Court, at which jury trials may be had as above provided, the Clerk of said court shall draw from the jury box the names of as many persons as the Judge of said court may deem necessary, not less than fourteen, nor more than twenty-four, to serve as petit jurors in said court; and at least two days before such drawing, the said Clerk shall give notice to the Judge of said court and to the Sheriff of the day and hour when such drawing shall take place.

Judge and Sheriff of Wayne County to attend drawing.

SEC. 38. At the time so appointed, it shall be the duty of said Judge, and of the Sheriff of Wayne County, or some Deputy Sheriff, to attend at the Clerk's office and witness said drawing of jurors, and if neither said Judge, Sheriff or Deputy Sheriff be present at the appointed time, the Clerk may adjourn such drawing to some certain hour on the next day, of which adjournment he shall forthwith give notice to said Judge and Sheriff.

Proceedings on drawing jurors.

SEC. 39. If at the time first appointed for such drawing, or at the adjourned time therefor, either said Judge, Sheriff or Deputy Sheriff shall be present, the Clerk shall proceed in such drawing as follows: he shall shake the jury box, so as fairly to mix the slips of paper deposited therein; shall then draw from said box publicly and in the presence of the officer or officers attending, as many strips of paper, containing the names of jurors written thereon, as may have been ordered by said Judge, and one of the attending officers shall keep a minute of such drawing, in which he shall enter the name on every strip of paper drawn, before any other such strip be drawn. If, after drawing the whole number required, the name of any person shall appear to have been drawn who is insane or dead, or has removed from the City of Detroit, to the knowledge of said Clerk or any attending officer, and entry of such fact shall be made on the minute of the drawing, the strip of paper containing his name shall be destroyed and another name shall then be drawn in the place of that destroyed, and entered on the minute of the drawing, and like proceedings shall be had as often as necessary, until the whole number of jurors required shall be drawn.

SEC. 40. The said minute of the drawing shall then be signed by the Clerk of said court and the attending officers, and filed by the Clerk in his office, and he shall immediately make out a *venire facias* and deliver the same to the Sheriff of Wayne County, which shall command him or any of his deputies to summon the persons therein named to be and appear in said court, at the terms thereof for which they were drawn, to serve as petit jurors, and not depart the same until discharged, under such penalty as the court may impose.

Minute of drawing jurors to be filed.

*Venire facias*

Who to serve.

SEC. 41. Said *venire facias* shall be served at least three days before the term of the court therein specified, by giving personal notice to each person therein named, or by leaving a written notice at his place of residence, with some person of proper age, and return thereof shall be made to said court at its opening, specifying those who were summoned, and the manner in which each person was notified.

*Venire facias* how served and return'd.

SEC. 42. Said court shall impose a fine on each person duly summoned to attend as a juror, who shall, without reasonable cause, neglect to attend, not exceeding five dollars for each day's non-attendance and neglect; but all persons who, under the general laws of the State, are exempted or may be excused from serving as jurors in the Circuit Courts,

Fines for neglect of jurors to attend.

Exemption.

shall be exempted and may be excused from serving as jurors in said Recorder's Court.

Proceedings when jurors excused.

SEC. 43. The Clerk of said court shall destroy the ballots of all persons excused from serving as jurors, on the ground of being exempted by law from such service; and the ballots of persons who did not appear and serve, which shall not have been destroyed, shall be returned to the jury box.

Ballots of persons attending as jurors to be deposited in box.

SEC. 44. The ballots of persons who shall attend and serve as jurors, shall be inclosed by the Clerk in an envelope, under seal, or deposited by him in a separate box and preserved; and if, at any subsequent drawing of a jury, a sufficient number of ballots shall not remain in the jury box to furnish the number of jurors required, after having drawn all the ballots therein, the ballots preserved by the Clerk as aforesaid shall be returned by him to the jury box and drawn in like manner as required above, until the required number of jurors is obtained.

Drawing jurors forthwith in certain cases.

SEC. 45. Whenever, for any cause, petit jurors shall not have been drawn or summoned to attend any term of said Recorder's Court, or a sufficient number of qualified jurors shall fail to appear, such court may, in its discretion, order a sufficient number of petit jurors to be forthwith drawn and summoned to attend such court; or said court may, by an order to be entered in its minutes, direct the Sheriff forthwith to summon so many good and qualified men of said city to serve as such jurors, as the case may require.

Duties of Sheriff in summoning jurors and making return.

SEC. 46. The Sheriff, on receiving a list of jurors drawn pursuant to the preceding section, or a copy of the order therein mentioned, shall proceed, as soon as possible, to summon such jurors forthwith to attend such court, and make return to said court of his doings, in the same manner as in the case of a *venire facias*.

Talesmen.

SEC. 47. When there shall not be jurors enough present to form a panel to any case, said court may direct the Sheriff to summon a sufficient number of persons having the qualifications of jurors, to complete the panel, from among the by-standers or the neighboring citizens; and the Sheriff shall immediately summon the number so ordered and return their names to said court.

SEC. 48. In all further proceedings touching jury trials, their incidents and all matters connected therewith, said Recorder's Court shall be governed, in the same manner as the Circuit Courts of the State, by the general laws thereof, which, so far as the same may apply, are hereby made applicable to said Recorder's Court, its officers and all proceedings therein, subject to the provisions of this act. General laws applicable to further proceedings.

SEC. 49. The Clerk of said court, on the first day of January in each year, or as soon thereafter as practicable, shall make to the Common Council a report, in writing, duly certified by him, showing the whole number of prosecutions by indictment, which number shall be also classified by the name or description of the offense; the whole number of prosecutions for offenses against this act or the ordinances and regulations of the Common Council, which shall be also classified in like manner, so far as practicable; the whole number of prosecutions, convictions, acquittals, cases dismissed and discontinued, and cases pending; the whole number of sentences passed; the whole number punished by fines and penalties; the whole number punished by imprisonment and confinement, which shall also be classified according to the prison, jail or other place of imprisonment or confinement; and the whole number held to bail for good behavior, and to keep the peace; and said report shall be published in the daily newspaper published by the printer for the city. Clerk to report to Common Council. Report, what to contain.

SEC. 50. The provisions of this chapter shall not go into effect until the second Tuesday in January, 1858; and the provisions of the present Charter of said city, relative to the Mayor's Court, shall continue in full force and effect until the Recorder's Court is organized, under this act. Provisions of this chapter to go into effect on the second Tuesday in January, 1858.

# CHAPTER VII.

## OPENING, ALTERING AND CLOSING STREETS.



Powers of Common Council as to streets.

Hinchman vs. City of Detroit, 9 Mich.

SECTION 1. The Common Council of the City of Detroit shall have full power to lay out, establish, open, extend, widen, straighten, alter, close, vacate, or abolish any highways, streets, avenues, lanes, alleys, public grounds, or spaces in said city, whenever they shall deem it a necessary public improvement, and private property may be taken therefor; but the necessity for using such property, the just compensation to be made for the same, and the damages arising to any person from the making of said improvement, shall be ascertained by a jury of twelve freeholders, residing in said city.

Resolution declaring improvement necessary; what to contain.

SEC. 2. Whenever the Common Council shall deem any such improvement necessary, they shall so declare by resolution, which shall be drawn by the City Attorney, and in said resolution shall describe the contemplated improvement; and if they intend to take private property therefor, they shall declare such intention, and describe such property, in said resolution, with particularity sufficient for an ordinary conveyance thereof; and further declare that they will, on some day to be named in said resolution, apply to the Recorder's Court of said city for the drawing of a jury, to ascertain the necessity for using the property intended to be taken, if it be intended to take any for such improvement, to ascertain the just damages and compensation which any person may be entitled to, if such intended improvement be made, and to apportion and assess such damages and compensation to and upon all lots, premises, and subdivisions thereof, which will be benefited by such improvement; and the time to be named for applying to said court, shall be on a day subsequent to the required publication of said resolution.

Notice of intended improvement; how given.

SEC. 3. The Common Council shall give notice of the intended improvement, and of their intended application to said court, by causing a copy of said resolution, certified by the Clerk of the city, to be published for four successive weeks, in the official daily newspaper of the city, and one other daily newspaper, published in said city, and the Marshal shall also give notice of said resolution, by delivering a notice thereof, with a copy of the same annexed, to the owner, or owners, or agent of any private property intended to be taken, if they can be found in said city, which notice shall be directed to them, or, if they cannot be found, by leaving the same at their place of residence in said city, with some person of proper age. If they, or their place of residence cannot be found, and such property be occupied, said notice and copy of said resolution shall be served by delivering the same to the occupant or occupants, or by leaving the same at their place of residence, within said city, with some person of proper age; but if the owner, or owners, or agent of such property, or their place of residence, cannot be found, and

Upon whom served.

it be not occupied, but they, their place of residence, and that of the occupant or occupants cannot be found, or if the owner or owners, occupant or occupants, be unknown, or non-residents of said city, then, in either of such cases, notice of said resolution may be given by posting the same, with the copy of said resolution, in some conspicuous place upon the property intended to be taken. The Marshal shall give notice of said resolution, as above directed, and make return of his doings, and of the manner of giving said notice as soon as practicable after the passage thereof, which return shall be made to said Recorder's Court, at least six days before the day appointed in said resolution for the hearing of said application, and all persons interested therein, after notice given in the manner aforesaid, shall take notice of, and be bound by all subsequent proceedings, without any further notices, except as herein otherwise provided.

Return of services.

When and where made.

Certified copy of resolution to be served on City Attorney.

SEC. 4. The Clerk of the city shall deliver to the City Attorney a certified copy of said resolution of the Common Council, whose duty it shall be to appear in said court, and make the application therein referred to, and conduct all further proceedings thereon in behalf of the Common Council.

Jurors.

SEC. 5. Upon the day designated in said resolution, or some other day, to be appointed by the court, and on filing a copy of said resolution, and an affidavit showing the required publication thereof, the Marshal shall attend said court, and write down the names of twenty-four disinterested freeholders, residing in said city, and who shall be approved by the court as such disinterested freeholders and residents, and as qualified to serve.

Summoning Jurors.

SEC. 6. Said Court shall then issue a writ of summons, commanding the Marshal to summon said twenty-four persons to be and appear in said court, to serve as jurors, on some day to be named therein, which shall not be less than seven days after the issuing thereof. The Marshal shall serve such summons at least three days before the return day thereof, and make return in the same manner as in the case of a summons for petit jurors of said court; and the persons thus summoned shall be bound to attend said court, and serve until discharged, and said court shall impose upon them a fine not exceeding five dollars for each day's non-attendance in court, or neglect to serve; but they may be exempted and excused by the court from serving, for the same reasons for which petit jurors may be exempted or excused.

Drawing jury.

SEC. 7. The names of the jurors in attendance, and who do not claim to be exempted, or are not excused from serving, shall then be written by the Clerk of the Court on separate slips of paper, of equal size and appearance, as near as practicable, and be deposited by him in a box having a lid, or cover. He shall then shake said box, so as thoroughly to mix said slips of paper, and shall then draw impartially, openly, and in the presence of the court, so many of the slips of paper, or ballots, containing names written thereon, one after another, as shall be sufficient to form a jury. The right of challenge shall be allowed, as in civil cases, under the laws of this State.

In case of insufficiency of ballots other persons to be summoned.

SEC. 8. If, in consequence of jurors being exempted, excused, or set aside, there shall not be in the box any ballots, or a sufficient number of ballots from which to draw the jury, the Marshal shall forthwith, under the order of the court, summon such number of persons as the court shall deem necessary, and may order to be and appear in said court, to serve as jurors, and the persons thus summoned shall be returned, be bound to attend said court and serve, and be competent to form the jury, in the same manner, and to the same effect as those first summoned.

First twelve appearing and approv'd to be jury and be sworn

SEC. 9. The first twelve persons who shall appear, as their names are drawn and called by the Clerk, or who are called by him when all the ballots have been drawn from the box, and shall be approved by the court as qualified, shall

10

be the jury, and be sworn to discharge their duties faithfully, and according to the best of their abilities. Said court shall then instruct said jury as to their duties, and the law applicable to the case, and deliver to them a copy of the resolution of the Common Council, as filed in said court, certified by the Clerk of said court; and the City Attorney shall give said jury legal advice and counsel concerning their duties, whenever requested.

Instructions to jury by Court and Attorney.

Jury to view.

SEC. 10. The jury shall go to the place of the intended improvement, and upon or as near as practicable to any property intended to be taken, and described in said resolution, or as the case may be, which will be damaged or benefited, if the intended improvement be made.

Duties of jury.

SEC. 11. Said jury shall then ascertain the necessity for using the property intended to be taken, if it be intended to take any for such improvement, and if they shall find in the affirmative, they shall next determine the just damages and compensation to be paid to the owner or owners of any property intended to be taken for, or that may be damaged by, the intended improvement, and award to the owner or owners thereof, such damages and compensation as they shall deem just. If such property shall be subject to a valid mortgage, lease, and agreement, or to either, and such facts shall be made to appear to the jury, then said jury shall apportion and award to the owners of such property, the parties in interest to such mortgage, lease, and agreement, or to either of them, such portions of the damages and compensation as they shall deem just. And in all cases where any such damages shall be awarded, except for the laying out, establishing, opening, widening, altering, or vacating an alley, or alleys, such damage shall be payable out of the city treasury, and the means therefor shall be raised from time to time, as may be necessary, with the general city taxes.

Certain damages payable out of city treasury.

Apportionment of damages among lots to be benefited.

SEC. 12. In cases of the laying out, establishing, opening, widening, altering, or vacating an alley, or alleys, said jury shall further proceed to apportion the total damages, and compensation to be paid for the proposed improvement among the lots of land, premises, or subdivisions thereof, within the block in which the alley in question is situated, and which will be benefited by the proposed improvement, apportioning and assessing the same upon the said lots, premises, or subdivisions thereof, as near as may be, in proportion as the same will be benefited by said improvement. The word "alley," as used in this chapter, shall be construed to mean only those ways or passages which bisect or divide the interior of a block. No alleys shall be opened, except upon a petition of the owners of a majority of the lots on the block or blocks to be intersected thereby, and upon security being given to indemnify the city against the expenses of opening said alleys.

Definition of word "alley."

People, vs. Jackson, 7 Mich, 432.

SEC. 13. Said jury, after completing the aforesaid duties, shall then make, in writing, and each shall sign the report to said court, of their doings, inclose the same in a sealed envelope, and file it in the office of the Clerk of said court, within thirty days after they were sworn.

Report of jury.

SEC. 14. In cases where said jury shall find such improvement to be necessary, they shall state, in their report, the just damages and compensation ascertained and awarded by them to the owner of any private property, or to any person claiming an interest therein, by virtue of any valid mortgage, lease, or agreement, to which such property may be subject, together with the names of such owner, or claimant, if known, and a description of the property intended to be taken. In case any damages and compensation be awarded to any person claiming an interest in such property, by virtue of a valid mortgage, lease, or agreement, to which such property may be subject, it shall be sufficient to state further, in such case, the name of such claimant, the date of such mortgage, lease, or agreement, or assignment thereof, if there be any, by virtue of which such claimant has an interest in the property intended to be taken.

Report, what to contain.

What further to contain.

SEC. 15. Said jury shall also, in the case provided by section twelve, state in their report what portions in amount of the total ascertained damages and compensation they have apportioned to and assessed upon any lot, premises, or subdivision thereof, which will be benefited by the intended improvement, together with the names of the owners thereof, if known, and a description of the same, and also what portion, if any, of the ascertained damages and compensation they have apportioned and assessed to the City of Detroit, in the case above provided for.

Confirmation of report.

SEC. 16. Said report may be confirmed by said court, at any term thereof, and the court shall appoint some day when it will consider said report and objections against the confirmation thereof, on the part of all persons interested therein, whereof the City Attorney shall give notice, by publishing the same in the official daily newspaper of said city, and in one other daily newspaper, published in said city, for six successive days, and he shall file in said court an affidavit of such publication, before the time appointed for considering said report. Said objections shall be filed with the Clerk, in writing, but may be argued, and the consideration of said report and objections may be adjourned, from time to time, until said report be confirmed, or otherwise disposed of, as herein provided.

Objection.

Report not to be annulled for matters of form.

SEC. 17. Said report shall not be annulled for objections as to matters of form; all objections shall be objections of law, and to matters of substance, but the damages and compensation to be paid to any person, or the portions thereof apportioned to, and assessed upon any lot of land, premises, or subdivision thereof, may be inquired into, if objected to as being excessively large or small.

If no objections filed, report to be confirmed.

SEC. 18. If no objections be filed, said report shall be confirmed; but if objections be filed, said court, after considering the same, shall, in its discretion, confirm or annul said report, or may refer it back to the same jury, for the purpose of reviewing all matters, and correcting all errors

Proceedings if objections are filed.

therein contained, and making any alteration thereof which said court may direct, or said jury may deem just or necessary, and thereon said jury shall review, correct, or alter said report, in manner aforesaid, and shall return and file the same, with the Clerk of said court, within five days after said report was referred back to them as aforesaid, and thereupon said court shall confirm or annul said report.

SEC. 19. If said report be annulled, or the jury cannot agree, or from death, sickness, or any other cause, shall fail to make a report within the thirty days required above, the court may, on the application of the City Attorney, designate some day in term, when another jury may be had, and such jury shall be obtained, drawn, summoned, returned, bound to attend and serve, have the same qualifications, be sworn, and, when sworn, have the same powers and duties as the first jury. The same proceedings, after they are sworn, shall be had by them, and by and in said court, as provided for above, after the first jury is sworn.

New Jury to be summoned in certain cases.

SEC. 20. If any juror, after being sworn, shall die, or from sickness be unable to discharge his duties, the court may appoint another person to serve in his place, who shall be sworn, and shall have the like qualifications, powers, and duties as those already sworn.

Vacancy in jury, how supplied.

SEC. 21. Any person, to whom damages and compensation may be awarded for any of his property, intended to be taken, or on account of the intended improvement, or to and upon whose property any portion of such damages and compensation may be apportioned and assessed, considering himself aggrieved, may appeal from the judgment of the Recorder's Court, confirming the report of the jury, to the Supreme Court, by filing, in writing, with the Clerk of said Recorder's Court, a notice of such appeal, and specification of the errors complained of, within five days after the confirmation, and serving, within the same time, a copy of said notice and specification of errors, on the City Attorney, and filing a bond in said Recorder's Court, to be approved by the Re-

Appeal.

Notice of specification of errors.

Bond on appeal.

Condition. corder, conditioned for the prosecution of said appeal, and the payment of all costs that may be awarded against the appellant, in case the judgment of confirmation of the Recorder's Court be affirmed.

Return to appeal. SEC. 22. In case of appeal, as above, it shall be the duty of the Clerk of said Recorder's Court, forthwith, or as soon as practicable, to transmit to the Supreme Court a certified copy of all the proceedings in the case, which may be filed in the office of any clerk of said court.

Duties of Supreme Court on appeal. SEC. 23. The Supreme Court, at any term thereof, shall, with the least practicable delay, hear and try the matter of said appeal, and may affirm or reverse the judgment of the Recorder's Court, confirming the report of the jury; but the same shall not be reversed for matter of form, nor for any errors, except errors of law, and only in regard to the appellant, or appellants. The court shall give judgment for reasonable costs and expenses in the matter of said appeal, and proceedings thereon to be taxed, and all costs and expenses awarded to the City of Detroit, in case of affirmation, shall be applied on and deducted from the damages and compensation, if any, to be paid to the appellant or appellants.

Remanding proceedings in certain cases. SEC. 24. If there be a reversal for any errors, which it is practicable for the Recorder's Court or said jury to correct, with due regard to the public interest and rights of individuals, the proceedings shall be remanded to said Recorder's Court, with direction that such error be corrected. Said Recorder's Court, at any term thereof, or (as the case may be) said jury, under the direction of said court, shall correct such error, and thereupon the report of the jury shall be confirmed by said Recorder's Court, without any further right of appeal.

Common Council may elect in certain cases to pay damages SEC. 25. In every case of annulment of the report of the jury, by the Recorder's Court, or reversal by the Supreme Court, the Common Council, in behalf of said city, may, by resolution, elect to pay the damages and compensation claimed by, or the assessment made upon the property of the objector, appellant, or appellants. On filing a certified copy of said resolution, in the Recorder's Court, within twenty days after the annulment or reversal, the report of said jury shall be reviewed and confirmed by said Recorder's Court, as to all persons interested therein, except the objector, appellant, or appellants, and without further right of appeal. If the Common Council do not elect, as above provided, all the proceedings shall be null and void, and no further proceedings shall be had, except in a case of reversal, when the proceedings may have been remanded to the Recorder's Court for the correction of certain errors, in which case such errors shall be corrected, and the report of the jury confirmed, as above provided.

Confirmation of report to be final.

SEC. 26. If the report of the jury be confirmed by the Recorder's Court, in any case above provided for, or if the judgment of confirmation be affirmed, on appeal to the Supreme Court, such confirmation shall be final and conclusive as to all persons interested therein; and the damages and compensation apportioned to, and assessed upon any lot of land, premises, or subdivision thereof, according to said report, as confirmed, shall be a lien thereon, from the time of the aforesaid confirmation, until they are paid and satisfied.

Certified copy of proceedings to be filed and recorded.

SEC. 27. When the report of the jury shall have been thus finally confirmed, or the judgment of confirmation affirmed by the Supreme Court, the Clerk of the Recorder's Court shall prepare a certified copy, under the seal of the court, of the report of the jury, as confirmed by the Recorder's Court, and of the order of the court, confirming the same, and the Clerk shall file said certified copy in the office of the Clerk of the city, who shall record the same at length, in a book to be provided, used and known as a book of street records. Such certified copy, such record, or a like copy, made and certified by the Clerk of the Recorder's Court, shall, in all courts and places, be presumptive evidence of the matters therein contained, and of the regularity of all proceedings, from the commencement thereof, to the order of the court confirming the report of the jury.

Amounts to be paid to City Treasurer.

SEC. 28. The amounts apportioned to and assessed upon all lots of land, premises, or subdivisions thereof, for the benefits they will receive, shall be paid to the Treasurer of said city, in case of confirmation of the report of the jury, as above provided, or in case the judgment of confirmation be affirmed by the Supreme Court, and may be collected, and said lots, premises, or subdivisions thereof may be sold therefor, in the same manner as in the case of collection or sale for assessments to pay the cost and expenses of paving streets.

Damages to be paid or tendered in sixty days.

SEC. 29. Within sixty days after the confirmation of the report of the jury, or after the judgment of confirmation shall, on appeal, be affirmed, the Common Council shall pay, or tender to the respective persons the several amounts of damages and compensation awarded to them, according to the report of the jury as confirmed, or elected as above provided for, to be paid by the Common Council; and in case any such person shall refuse the same, be unknown, or a non-resident of said city, or for any reason incapacitated from receiving his or her amount, or the right thereto be disputed or doubtful, the Common Council may deposit the amount awarded in such case, or elected to be paid by the Common Council, in the treasury of the city, to the credit of any person entitled thereto, and shall, on demand, pay the same over to any person competent and entitled to receive it.

Damages to be deposited in certain cases with treasurer.

Upon payment, tender or deposit, to become public highway.

SEC. 30. Upon such payment, tender, or deposit in the city treasury, the same shall become a public highway, and the Common Council may enter upon, take possession of, and convert the same to the uses and purposes for which it has been taken. A certificate of the City Treasurer of such tender, payment, or deposit, or record thereof, in the book of street records, or certified copy of such record, shall, in all courts and places, be presumptive evidence of the facts therein stated, of the vesting of the fee of the property taken in the City of Detroit, and of the right of the Common Council to take possession of and convert the same to the uses for which it has been taken.

SEC. 31. In all cases where any real estate, subject to any lease or agreement, shall be taken as aforesaid, all the covenants and stipulations contained therein shall cease, determine, and be discharged, upon the final confirmation of the report of the jury, or upon the affirmation by the Supreme Court of the judgment of confirmation. If a part, only, of such real estate be taken, said covenants and stipulations shall cease, determine, and be discharged only as to such part; and the Recorder's Court, on application of any party in interest to such lease or agreement, and after a notice thereof of eight days, in writing, to the other parties in interest, may appoint three disinterested residents and freeholders of said city, commissioners, to determine the rents and payments to be thereafter paid, and the covenants, stipulations, or conditions thereafter to be performed under such lease or agreement, in respect to the residue or part of such real estate not taken. Said commissioners shall, before entering on their duties, take and subscribe an oath, to be administered by the court, faithfully to discharge their duties, which oath shall be filed in said court. Said three commissioners shall make and sign a report, in writing, of their doings, to said court, which shall be filed therein within thirty days after their appointment, and said report, on being confirmed by the court, shall be binding and conclusive on the parties in interest to such lease or agreement.

Upon confirmation of report, stipulations in lease or agreem'ts to cease.

Commiss'ers to apportion rents in certain cases.

Duties of Commissioners.

SEC. 32. The Common Council shall pay said jury such compensation for their services as they may deem just, and they shall have power to abandon or discontinue proceedings, under this chapter, in said Recorder's Court, at any time before the final confirmation of the report of the jury.

Compensation of Jury.

Common Council may abandon proceedings.

SEC. 33. For the purpose of introducing a greater uniformity in the laying out the land in said city into public streets and blocks, and to restrain persons from laying out

Commission on plan of city.

such streets and blocks in a manner prejudicial to the interest of the city, there shall be constituted a Board of Commissioners, upon the plan of the city, consisting of three persons, to be appointed by the Common Council, on the nomination of the Mayor, and no land within the limits of said city shall be laid out into blocks and public streets, without the consent and approval of a majority of said Commissioners, in writing, entered upon a plan of said land so laid out, which plan, duly acknowledged, and with said approval, in writing, thereon indorsed, shall be recorded in the Register's office for the County of Wayne: *Provided, however*, In cases where a parcel of land lies between parcels of land duly laid out by plats, now on record, whose streets do not correspond in direction or size, the power of control shall not be so exercised over the platting of such intermediate parcel in order to produce such correspondence, as to essentially diminish their value.

Land not to be laid out into blocks and streets without consent of Commissioners.

Proviso.

Clerk of Board; plans to be deposited with Clerk

SEC. 34. The City Clerk shall act as the Clerk of said Board, and plans for the approval of said Commissioners, may be deposited with said Clerk for their action thereon, and if approved, a copy thereof shall be filed with said Clerk, by the person making or laying out the same.

Plans not acknowledged and recorded to be of no validity without approval of Commissioners.

SEC. 35. Any plans for laying out into public streets and blocks, now existing in said city, and not acknowledged and recorded according to law, shall be of no validity until they receive the approval of said Commissioners, as hereinbefore provided. But the platting and recording of any blocks, lots, squares, lanes, alleys, parks, or public places within said city, shall be a full and irrevocable dedication of the same to the public for the uses and purposes specified or named upon any such record, plat, or plan; any such plats or plans, now of record, shall be, and be evidence of dedication, as hereinbefore provided, unless reclaimed of record within thirty days after this act shall take effect. [*As amended by Section* 20 *of the Act of* 1861.

SEC. 36. If a vacancy occurs in the office of said Commissioners, or either of them, it may be filled by the Common Council, on the nomination of the Mayor. Vacancies, how filled.

SEC. 37. Said Commissioners shall receive no compensation for their services. No compensation.

---

# CHAPTER VIII.

## TAXATION AND FINANCE.



SECTION 1. The revenues and moneys of the corporation shall be divided into the following funds, viz.: Funds.

1st. General Fund, which shall be appropriated to defray the expenses of the City of Detroit, for the payment of which out of some other fund, no provision is herein made. Gener'l Fund

Contingent. 2d. Contingent Fund, to defray the contingent expenses of said city.

Interest. 3d. Interest Fund, to pay the interest on the funded debt of said city.

Sinki'g Fund 4th. Sinking Fund, to pay the funded debt of said city.

Fire Department Fund. 5th. Fire Department Fund, to defray the expenses of purchasing lots, erecting engine houses thereon, purchasing engines and other fire apparatus, and all other expenses necessary to maintain the Fire Department of said city.

Poor Fund. 6th. Poor Fund, to defray the expenses of providing for and taking care of the poor of said city.

Gener'l Road Fund. 7th. General Road Fund, to defray the expenses of repairing paved streets and alleys, and of grading, paving and improving the highways, streets and alleys of said city, in front of or adjacent to the property of the corporation.

District Road Fund. 8th. District Road Fund for each ward of the city, to defray the expenses of working, repairing, cleaning, and improving the highways, streets, and alleys in the ward for which such District Road Fund is constituted and raised.

Sewer Fund. 9th. Sewer Fund, to defray the expenses of constructing sewers in said city.

Street Opening Fund. 10th. Street Opening Fund, to defray the expenses of opening, widening, vacating, altering, straightening, extending or abolishing any highways, streets or avenues in said city, under the provisions of chapter seven of this act.

Street Paving Fund. 11th. Street Paving Fund, to defray the expenses of grading, paving and graveling, macadamising or planking highways, streets, alleys, side-walks and cross-walks in front of or adjacent to private property, and of putting curb-stones and culverts therein.

Public Building Fund. 12th. Public Building Fund, for purchasing any real estate for the erection thereon of any public buildings, and to defray the expenses of erecting, repairing and preserving such public buildings as the Common Council is authorized to erect and maintain, and are not herein otherwise provided for, which fund shall, from time to time, be divided into Special

Building Funds, to defray the expenses of erecting, repairing and preserving the particular building or buildings for which such Special Building Fund may be constituted or raised.

13th. Recorder's Court Fund, to maintain the Recorder's Court. Recorder's Court Fund.

14th. Such other funds as the Common Council may constitute for special purposes, not inconsistent with, nor to be taken from any of the funds above constituted or raised. Other Funds.

SEC. 2. The Common Council shall have power annually to levy, assess and collect taxes, not exceeding one per cent. on the assessed value of all real and personal estate in said city, made taxable by the laws of this State, in order to defray the expenses, and for the purposes for which the General Fund, Contingent Fund, Fire Department Fund, Poor Fund, General Road Fund and Recorder's Court Fund are constituted as above. Powers of Council to collect. Taxes for certain funds.

SEC. 3. The Common Council shall also have power annually to levy, assess and collect taxes on the assessed value of all real and personal estate in each ward of said city, made taxable by the laws of this State, in order to defray the expenses, and for the purposes for which the District Road Fund is constituted as above: *Provided*, That such taxes shall not exceed in amount, the rates of township road or highway taxes as now or hereafter established by the laws of this State. For District Road Fund.

SEC. 4. The Common Council shall also have power annually to levy, assess and collect taxes, not exceeding thirty thousand dollars, on the assessed value of all real and personal estate in said city, made taxable by the laws of this State, in order to defray the expenses of constructing sewers, and for the purposes for which the Sewer Fund is constituted as above. For Sewer Fund.

SEC. 5. Before any taxes shall be levied, as aforesaid, for the purposes of the General Fund, Contingent Fund, General Road Fund, Street Opening Fund, District Road Fund, Fire Department Fund, Poor Fund, Sewer Fund, and Recorder's Controller to present estimate.

Court Fund, the Controller shall present to the Common Council, in writing, his estimate of the amount of taxes, which, in his opinion, it may be necessary to raise for the ensuing year, for the purposes of said fund; shall state therein the amount estimated for the purposes of each of said funds, and also an estimate of the entire proposed expenditures for said year, whether the same is to be raised by tax, by loan, or by special assessment, and said estimate shall be published in the official paper of the city, and shall, at the same time, give to the Common Council any information in his power, and which they may request, concerning the finances of said city. The Common Council, after revising or altering said estimate, but not so as to exceed the aggregate taxes hereby authorized to be levied, shall direct the Mayor or acting Mayor to call a public meeting of the citizens of said city, to take into consideration the taxes proposed to be raised and specified in said estimate, by publishing notice thereof in one or more daily newspapers published in said city, for not less than three successive days, and posting the same in conspicuous places in said city, at least three days prior to the time of the meeting, which notice shall contain the substance of said estimate. Said meeting shall transact the business for which it was called. If a majority of the citizens present shall consent to the levying of the taxes specified in said estimate, then the Common Council shall proceed to levy, assess and collect the same, or such part thereof as may have been consented to; but if said meeting shall not consent to the levying of said taxes, the said Common Council may call a second meeting of said citizens in the same manner, and which shall have the same power as the first meeting hereinbefore provided for.

Public meeting to vote taxes.

Second meeting.

Taxes for Interest Fund.

SEC. 6. The Common Council shall annually levy, assess and collect on the assessed value of all the real and personal estate in said city, made taxable by the laws of this State, taxes for the purposes of the interest fund, not exceeding, in amount, a sufficient sum to pay the interest, accrued or to accrue on the funded debt of said city, for the year for which such taxes are levied; and also taxes not less than five, nor more than ten thousand dollars, for the purposes of the sinking fund.

Special Sewer Tax.

SEC. 7. The Common Council shall also have power annually to levy, assess and collect a tax or assessment on all lots, premises and subdivisions, thereof drained by private sewers or drains, leading into or connected with any public sewer, or drain, which tax shall be one dollar and fifty cents on every lot, premises or subdivision thereof having a cellar, fifty cents if there be no cellar thereon, and such sums as the Common Council may fix for all lots and establishments drained as aforesaid, and requiring an unusual or extraordinary amount of drainage. Said tax or assessment shall be credited to the sewer fund, and applied to the repairing of sewers and drains, and if the same be more than is required for such purpose, the surplus may be applied to the construction of sewers and drains.

Tax for grading, paving, etc.

Woodbridge vs. Detroit, 8 Mich. 272.

Proviso.

SEC. 8. The Common Council shall also have power from time to time to levy, assess and collect a tax or assessment on all lots, premises or subdivisions thereof, sufficient to defray the expenses of grading and paving, graveling, macadamizing or planking any highway, avenue, street, lane, alley, or crosswalk in said city, in front of or adjacent to such lots, premises or subdivisions thereof, and of putting curb-stones and culverts therein, the proceeds of which tax or assessment shall be credited to the street paving fund : *Provided*, That such tax or assessment shall not, in any one year exceed, in the aggregate, the sum of fifty thousand dollars, except upon the petition of the holders of a majority of the property upon any alley, street, block or square which the petitioners may desire paved; such grading, paving, graveling, macadamizing and putting in of curb-stones and culverts shall be commenced and completed, and all contracts therefor shall require the same to be commenced and completed within the six months next preceding the first day of December of the year in which such contract shall be made, but it shall be lawful for the Common Council to extend the time for the completion of any such contract for work which may have been commenced in good faith and not fully completed by the time above mentioned. [*As amended by Sec.* 22 *of the act of* 1861.]

Loans for Public Building fund.

SEC. 9. The Common Council shall also have power to provide money for the public building fund, by loaning, upon the faith and credit of said city, and upon the best terms that can be made, a sum of money not exceeding three hundred thousand dollars, and to issue the bonds of said city to an amount not exceeding that sum, pledging its faith and credit for the payment of the principal and interest, but said bonds shall not be negotiated at less than their par value. Said bonds shall be denominated "Public Building Stock of the City of Detroit," shall be regularly dated and numbered in the order of their issue; shall be for sums not less than five hundred dollars each; shall bear interest not exceeding seven per cent. per annum; shall be payable in not less than twenty years from date; shall be issued under the seal of the corporation, signed by the Mayor, and countersigned by the Controller. The Controller shall keep an accurate record of said bonds, showing the class of indebtedness to which they belong, the number, date, and amount of each bond, its rate of interest, when and where the same is payable, and the person to whom it is issued. The proceeds of said bonds shall be paid to the Treasurer, and be credited to the public building fund, and applied exclusively to the purposes for which said fund is constituted as above. [*As amended by Sec.* 23 *of the act of* 1861.

Consent of public meeting required for issue of bonds for public building fund.

SEC. 10. No bonds shall be issued as aforesaid for the purposes of the public building fund, until a public meeting of the citizens of said city shall have been called and held to consider the subject of constructing a public building for such purpose as the Common Council may propose, which meeting shall be called and may be held in the manner above prescribed for calling and holding in relation to the levying of taxes. The Common Council shall cause to be presented to said meeting, by the Controller, an estimate of the necessary cost of purshasing the necessary real estate for the erection thereon of any building and expense of the building proposed to be constructed. If a majority of the citizens present shall consent to the purchase of such real estate, and construction of a building for the purpose proposed, and to the estimate presented, or any part thereof, the Common Council shall then be authorized to contract for the purchase of such real estate and for the construction of said building, at a cost and expense not exceeding in amount, the estimate or part thereof thus consented to, and to expend thereon, borrow money and issue bonds as above provided. [*As Amended by Section* 23 *of the Act of* 1861.

Public works not provided for; how and when to be let.

SEC. 11. No contract shall be let or entered into for the construction of any public work within said city, not herein otherwise provided for, and no such public work shall be commenced, until it shall have been approved by the Common Council, and a tax or assessment levied to defray the cost and expense thereof; and no such public work shall be paid for or contracted to be paid for, except out of the proceeds of the tax or assessment thus levied.

No contract for over $200 to be let except to the lowest bidder.

SEC. 12. No contract for the purchase of any real estate, or for the construction of any public building, sewer, paving, graveling, planking, macadamizing, or for the construction of any public work whatever, or for any work to be done, or for purchasing or furnishing any material, printing or supplies for said corporation, if the purchase of said real estate, or the expense of such construction, repairs, work, materials, or supplies shall exceed two hundred dollars, shall be let, or entered into, except to and with the lowest responsible bidder, with adequate security, and as to such work or material, requiring mechanical skill, to and with practical mechanics, and as to such other work, supplies or material not requiring mechanical skill, to and with such persons as shall be deemed competent for the performance of any such contract, and not until advertised proposals and specifications therefor shall have been duly published in at least one daily newspaper published in said city, and for such period as the Common Council shall prescribe. And no bids shall be accepted from, or contract awarded to, any person who is in arrears to the corporation upon debt or contract, or who is a defaulter as security, or otherwise, upon any obligation to the corporation, or who shall be in other respects disqualified according to the provisions of this act.

Evidence of debt; for what issued.

SEC. 13. No loan, bond, or other evidence of debt, not expressly authorized by this act, or any act hereby continued in force, shall be made or issued by the Common Council or any officer of the corporation : *Provided, however*, That the Common Council may issue new bonds for the refunding of bonds and evidences of debt already issued; and the proper officer of the corporation may draw and issue orders on the Treasurer for the necessary and current expenses of the city.

Council may authorize Controller to borrow money.

SEC. 14. The Common Council shall not have authority to borrow, except as herein before provided, any sums of money whatever, on the credit of the corporation, but may authorize the Controller to borrow from time to time on such credit, in anticipation of the revenues of the corporation for the current fiscal year, and not to exceed such revenues in amount, such sums as may be necessary to meet the expenditures under the appropriations for the current fiscal year.

New bonds; what to show and how issued.

SEC. 15. All new bonds, issued for the refunding of bonds and evidences of debt before issued, shall show the class of indebtedness to which they belong; be issued on the best terms that can be made ; be regularly dated and numbered in the order of their issuance; shall be for sums not less than five hundred dollars each; shall be issued under the seal of the corporation, signed by the Mayor, and countersigned by the Controller. The Controller shall keep an accurate record, showing the class of indebtedness to which they belong, the number, date and amount of each bond, its rate of interest,

Controller to keep record.

when and where the same is payable, and the person to whom it is issued, and showing also what bonds or evidences of debt have been thereby refunded.

Refunded bonds to be canceled and destroyed.

SEC. 16. All bonds and evidences of debt, when refunded, shall be canceled and destroyed by the Treasurer, in the presence of the Controller and a special committee of the Common Council appointed for the purpose. He shall record and keep an accurate description of all bonds and evidences of debt thus canceled and destroyed.

Bonds void when issued contrary to this act.

SEC. 17. All bonds and evidences of debt issued, and all contracts made or entered into contrary to or not authorized by the provisions of this act, shall be absolutely void. The Common Council shall incur no expenses and create or pay no debt or liability contrary to or not authorized by the provisions of this act, and shall not appropriate or use the property or moneys of the corporation, except as authorized by and in pursuance of law.

No illegal claim to be paid.

SEC. 18. No claim or demand against the corporation shall be allowed or paid, or warrant on the treasury issued therefor, if the same be contrary to, or is not authorized by law, and no additional allowance beyond the legal claim under any contract with the corporation, or for any service on its account, or in its employment, shall be allowed. No warrant on the treasury shall be drawn for any claim or demand for the payment of which there is no money in the treasury raised or received for such purpose, or after the fund constituted and raised therefor has been exhausted by warrants previously drawn thereon, or by appropriations, liabilities, debts and expenses actually made, incurred or contracted for, and to be paid out of such fund.

No warrant to be drawn when there is no money in Treasury.

No money to be paid from treasury except on warrant.

SEC. 19. No moneys shall be paid out of the treasury, except upon a warrant signed by the Controller, and approved or authorized by the Common Council in pursuance of law. Such warrant shall specify the purpose for which the amount thereof is to be paid, with sufficient clearness to indicate the particular fund constituted or raised therefor,

What warrant to contain and how indorsed.

shall have indorsed thereon the name of the particular fund out of which it is payable, and shall be paid from the fund constituted for such purpose, and from no other.

Claim to be accompanied by affidavit.

SEC. 20. No claim against the corporation shall be audited or paid unless accompanied by the affidavit of the claimant, (if such affidavit be required by the Controller,) that the service, labor or materials upon which such claim is based, have been actually rendered, performed or furnished; that said claim is justly due, and that no part thereof has been paid, except as to the credits, if any, set forth in the account therefor.

Drafts on funds limited.

SEC. 21. The Common Council shall not, by warrant, draft or order on the treasury, or by any form of contract, create any liability or expense, for the payment of which any particular fund is constituted as above, to a greater amount in the aggregate, for any one year, than the amount of moneys raised for and paid into such fund for the year. All warrants, drafts, orders, and contracts payable under this act, out of any particular fund, and issued or made after the moneys raised for and paid into such fund shall have been exhausted by payments therefrom, or liabilities created and to be paid out of said fund, shall be absolutely void as against the corporation.

Officers not to be interested in any contract with city.

SEC. 22. No contract or agreement, written or verbal, to which the corporation shall be a party, or to which any officer or board thereof shall officially be a party, for the construction of any pavement, building, sewer, or performance of any public work whatsoever, or contract, or agreement, requiring the expenditure, receipt, or disposition of money or property, by the corporation, of any officer or board thereof, or creating any debt or liability, shall be let, or entered into, either directly or indirectly, with any member of the Common Council, or other officer of the corporation, either as principal or surety, and any such contract or agreement thus let or entered into, shall be absolutely void: *Provided, however*, That nothing herein contained shall prevent

Proviso.

the Overseer of Highways, of any ward, from contracting with the corporation for cleaning, repairing, or improving the streets in their wards respectively. [*As amended by Section* 25 *of the Act of* 1861.

SEC. 23. No ordinance, resolution, or proceeding of the Common Council, imposing taxes or assessments, or requiring the payment, expenditure, or disposition of money or property, or creating any debt or liability therefor, and no other ordinance shall be passed at the same meeting at which it was introduced, unless by unanimous consent, or at a special meeting called therefor, and every such ordinance, resolution, or proceeding shall be passed by yeas and nays, to be entered on the record. No ordinance, etc., to be passed at meeting at which it was introduced.

SEC. 24. The Common Council shall determine the fiscal year, and within one month after the end thereof, the Controller shall render to the Common Council a full, complete, and detailed statement, with tabular lists, of all moneys received and expended by the corporation for the preceding fiscal year, showing on what account they were received and expended, to what funds they were credited, and out of what funds they were paid, and classifying each receipt and expenditure under its appropriate head. In such statement he shall also give, by tabular lists and otherwise, such general information as may be necessary for an understanding of the pecuniary resources and liabilities of said city, and of the condition of each fund, and may make such recommendations concerning the same, as the interests of said city may require. The Common Council shall cause said statement to be published in the daily newspaper, published by the printer for said city, and in such other paper or papers as the Common Council may direct. Fiscal year. Controller's report. What to contain. To be published.

SEC. 25. The Common Council and the Controller, or either, may, at any time, require from the various officers and boards of the corporation, and it shall be their duty to furnish, when required, and in such form as shall be required, full and particular estimates, in detail, of the expenses of Controller or Council may require estimates and accounts from officers and boards.

their offices or departments for the current or next ensuing fiscal year, and also full and particular accounts, in detail, of their expenses for any past year, or for any part thereof.

Money may be put in bank.

SEC. 26. The Common Council shall have power to contract with any safe bank or banks, for the safe keeping of the public moneys, and for the receipt of interest, at a rate not exceeding that established by law, upon such moneys of the corporation deposited with such bank or banks, and to be drawn on account current from such bank or banks, by the corporation, or proper officer thereof, and such interest shall belong and be credited to the sinking fund.

Committee for negotiation of loans.

SEC. 27. The Mayor, Controller, and Chairman of the Committee on Ways and Means, shall be a committee for the negotiation of all loans authorized by this act, except as to any loans to be made by the Controller, under the authority of the Common Council, as above provided; and a majority of said committee shall have power to make such negotiation, subject to the approval of the Common Council.

Taxes, to what fund credited.

SEC. 28. All taxes and moneys raised, received, or appropriated for the purpose of any particular fund, shall be paid in and credited to such particular fund; and all taxes and moneys not raised, received, or appropriated for the purpose of any particular fund, shall be paid in and credited to the general fund, or such other fund as the Common Council shall direct.

Moneys, how applied.

SEC. 29. The moneys belonging to the several funds of the corporation, and all taxes and moneys raised, received, or appropriated for the purposes thereof, shall be applied to the purposes for which said funds are respectively constituted, as above; and for which said taxes and moneys are raised, received, or appropriated: *Provided, however*, That if, from any cause, there shall be, at the end of any fiscal year, a surplus in any other than the public building fund, the district road fund, for each ward, and the sinking fund, over and above the actual or estimated cost of any work for which the money of any fund was specifically raised, such surplus

Proviso.

shall be transferred and credited, by the Treasurer, to said sinking fund, at the end of such fiscal year, whenever there shall not be sufficient moneys therein to pay the outstanding funded debt of said city.

Moneys not to be transferred from one fund to another.

SEC. 30. Moneys shall not be transferred from one fund to another, and the moneys received and properly belonging to one fund, shall not be credited to any other, or different fund, except to the sinking fund, as above provided; but the Controller shall have the power to divide the several funds above constituted into special funds, to defray special expenses, belonging to the same class of expenses, for the payment of which said several funds are above constituted.

Funds may be divided.

Board of Commissioners of Sinking Fund.

SEC. 31. The Mayor, Controller, Treasurer, and Committee on Ways and Means, and their successors in office, by virtue of their offices, shall be a Board of Commissioners of the sinking fund. They shall, from time to time, upon the best terms they can make, purchase or pay the outstanding funded debt of said city, or such part thereof as they may be able to purchase or pay, until the same be fully purchased up, or paid; and all bonds and evidences of debt, thus purchased or paid, shall be delivered to the Treasurer, and shall become and be the property of the Commissioners of the sinking fund, and the interest thereon shall be credited and belong to the sinking fund; and whenever they cannot arrange for purchasing or paying the said debt, or any part thereof, they shall, temporarily, and until they can so arrange, invest the moneys belonging to said sinking fund in such securities, paying an interest of not less than seven per cent., as they may deem safe and advisable. Said Commissioners shall, from time to time, and whenever requested by the Common Council, make report of their doings, which report shall be made to the Common Council, referred to and filed with the Controller, and recorded by him in some proper book, to be provided for the purpose.

Duties of Board.

Meetings of Board.

SEC. 32. Said Board of Commissioners of the sinking fund shall be a board of the corporation, within the meaning of this act, and shall be subject to the provisions of any existing or future ordinances of said city, relative to the sinking fund. They shall meet, from time to time, for the transaction of business, and may adopt rules of proceeding at their meetings. A majority of the whole board shall be a quorum for the transaction of business, but they shall not purchase in, or pay the outstanding funded debt of said city, or invest any of the moneys belonging to the sinking fund, as above provided, except under a resolution for such purpose, passed and approved by the vote of a majority of the whole board, and by yeas and nays, to be entered of record.

Who to preside.

The Mayor, or, in case of his absence, some member, to be appointed by those present, shall preside at their meetings.

Secretary, his duty.

They shall appoint one of their members Secretary of the Board, whose duty it shall be to keep a true record of its doings.

Treasurer to have custody of Sinking Fund.

SEC. 33. The Treasurer shall have the custody of all moneys, securities, and evidences of value, belonging or pertaining to the sinking fund, and shall pay out the moneys of said fund only by order of the Commissioners, or a majority thereof, and upon the warrant of the Controller.

Pledge for payment of moneys borrowed.

SEC. 34. The faith and property of the City of Detroit shall remain pledged for the final payment of all bonds issued, and of all moneys borrowed by authority of, and in accordance with this or any other act of the Legislature of this State.

Officer converting money of corporation to be deemed guilty of malfeasance in office.

SEC. 35. If any officer of the corporation shall, directly or indirectly, appropriate or convert any of the moneys, securities, evidences of value, or any property whatsoever, belonging to the corporation, or any board thereof, to his own use, or shall, directly or indirectly, and knowingly, appropriate or convert the same to any other purpose than that for which such moneys, securities, evidences of value, or property may have been appropriated, raised, or received, or to any purpose not authorized by law, he shall be deemed guilty of willful and corrupt malfeasance in office, and may be prosecuted, tried, and convicted therefor, and on conviction, may be punished by fine not exceeding one thousand dollars, and imprisonment in the State prison, jail of Wayne County, or jail of said city, not exceeding three years, or either, in the discretion of the court. Punishment.

SEC. 36. The expenses of constructing and repairing plank crosswalks, in the several wards, shall be defrayed from the district road fund, mentioned in subdivision eight, of section one, of this chapter. [*Added by Section* 21 *of the Act of* 1861. Plank crosswalks, how paid for.

---

# CHAPTER IX.

## ASSESSMENT OF TAXES AND THEIR COLLECTION.



SECTION 1. There shall be an assessor appointed by the Common Council, upon the recommendation of the Mayor, who shall hold his office for the term of three years, and Assessor; term of office.

shall devote his whole time to the service of the city, in connection with the duties of his office, with power to appoint two assistants, and shall receive such compensation as the Common Council may determine.

Compensation.

Duties of Assessor in making assessments.

SEC. 2. (*See Note B.*) The said Assessor, or Assessors shall, between the first days of January and April in each year, assess all the real and personal property, subject to assessment or taxation by the laws of the State, within the limits of each ward respectively, of said city; and the said Assessor or Assessors shall so discriminate in assessing said tax, as not to impose upon the rural portions those expenses which belong exclusively to the built portions of the city; for which purpose, the Assessor or Assessors may, in his or their discretion, distinguish in their assessments what properties are within agricultural or rural sections, not having the benefit of lighting, watering, watching, and other expenditures, for purposes exclusively belonging to the built and densely populated portions of the city, and all lands within said agricultural or rural districts, exclusively used for the purpose of cultivation, pasture, meadow, woodland, or farming, may, in the discretion of the Assessor, be assessed as farm land, at their cash value; and said Assessor or Assessors shall, within the same period, make out and complete the assessment rolls, one for each ward respectively, in books to be provided for that purpose by the Common Council, and to be delivered to said assessor on or before the first day of January in each year. The action of the Assessor or Assessors shall at all times be subject to the correction and revision of the Board of Review and the Common Council of the

---

NOTE B.—The following is Section two, as originally enacted, in 1857:

SEC. 2. The said assessor shall, between the first days of January and April, in each year, assess all the real and personal property subject to assessment or taxation by the laws of this State, within the limits of each ward respectively, of said city, and shall, within the same period, make out and complete the assessment rolls, one for each ward respectively, in books to be provided for that purpose, by the Common Council, and to be delivered to said Assessor on or before the first day of January in each year: *Provided, however*, That the assessment of real and personal property made in the year eighteen hundred and fifty-six, shall be and remain the basis of taxation within said city for the year one thousand eight hundred and fifty-seven, and until the assessment for the year 1858 shall have been made out.

City of Detroit, as provided for in the charter of the city. [*As amended. See Laws of* 1859, *p.* 1057.

SEC. 3. The Assessor, together with the two Aldermen of each ward of the City of Detroit, shall be, and are hereby vested with the powers and duties of Supervisors, as provided by the laws of this State, not inconsistent with the provisions of this chapter, and said Assessor and Aldermen shall attend the annual session of the Board of Supervisors of the County of Wayne, in October, and all other sessions thereof, and shall represent the interests of this corporation in said Board. [*As Amended. See Laws of* 1859, *p.* 342.

Assessors and Aldermen to have powers of supervisors.

SEC. 4. If any lot or lots shall lie partly in two or more wards, the same shall be assessed in the ward where the greater proportion of such lot or lots is situated, and the said Assessor shall describe all lands, tenements, and subdivisions thereof, subject to assessment or tax in said city, by refering to the number and section of the lot, and the owner or occupant thereof, and if the number and section of any lot, or the owner or occupant thereof cannot be ascertained, then by such other sufficient description as such Assessor may deem proper; and if, by mistake or otherwise, any person may be improperly designated as the owner of any lot, tenement, or premises, such assessment or tax shall not, for that cause be vitiated, but the same shall be a lien on such lot, tenement, or premises, and collected as in other cases.

Proceedings where lots lie in two or more wards.

SEC. 5. The Assessor shall have power and authority to demand of every person owning or having charge, as agent or otherwise, of any property taxable in any ward, a list of such property, with such description as will enable him to assess the same, which demand may be made in writing, and by delivering the same to such person, or by leaving the same at his place of residence, with some person of proper years and discretion, and if the person of whom such demand may be made, shall not, within ten days thereafter, deliver to such assessor a list of the property in said ward belonging to him or her, or under his or her charge, with a

Assessor may demand list of owner or agent.

correct description of the same, or if he shall omit any such property in the list delivered, said Assessor shall have power, and it shall be his duty, to assess such property, upon such knowledge or information, as may be satisfactory to him, at its cash value, and according to his best judgment and discretion.

Board of Review; how appointed.

SEC. 6. A Board of Review shall, on the nomination of the Mayor, be appointed by the Common Council. Said Board shall consist of three resident property holders of said city, who shall hold their office for the term of three years, except that the three persons first appointed, which shall be immediately after this act shall take effect, shall hold their offices respectively for the term of one, two, and three years, as shall be determined by lot, on the first meeting of said Board, and thereafter one member of said Board shall be appointed each year, for the term of three years, as hereinbefore provided. The session of the Board of Review shall be held at the Assessor's office, in said city, and shall commence on the first Monday in April, in each year, and continue from day to day until all of said assessment rolls have been fully and carefully reviewed, corrected, and approved, which shall be on or before the fifteenth day of May. The Board of Review shall have power, and it shall be their duty, to equalize, alter, amend, and correct any assessment or valuation, and to place upon the assessment roll of the proper ward, any taxable property, real or personal, not already assessed, held, or owned by any person or persons, and to strike from said rolls any property, real or personal, wrongfully thereon, but no assessment shall be increased or made by said Board without notice to the person or persons affected thereby, either verbal, or personal, or written, or printed, and left at the usual residence of such person, if a resident, and if a non-resident, by a publication in some daily newspaper published in said city. Any person considering himself aggrieved by reason of any assessment, may complain thereof, verbally or in writing, before the Board of

Session of; where held.

Powers and duties.

Review, and on sufficient cause being shown by the affidavit of such person, or by other evidence, to the satisfaction of such Board, they shall review the assessment complained of, and may alter or correct the same as to the person charged thereby, the property described therein, and the estimated value thereof. The concurrence of a majority of the Board shall be sufficient to decide any question of altering or correcting any assessment complained of. The Board, or a majority of them, having completed the review and correction of their assessment rolls, shall respectively sign and return the same to the Common Council. The members of said Board shall receive such compensation for their services as shall be prescribed by the Common Council. [*As amended by Section* 26 *of the Act of* 1861.

Compensation.

SEC. 7. At the meeting of the Board of Review, as required by the preceding section, they shall have the same power to review, correct, and equalize the assessment rolls of the several wards, which Supervisors now or hereafter may have, by law, to review, correct, and equalize the assessment rolls of townships in the respective counties of this State.

Board of Review to have same power as Board of Supervisors.

SEC. 8. The City Clerk shall cause a notice to the tax payers of said city to be published in the daily newspaper, published by the printer for the city, and in one other daily newspaper published in said city, for two weeks prior to the time of any meeting of the said Board of Review, stating the time and place of meeting of said Board, and the object for which it will meet, which notice shall be continued on each publication day of said papers, during the session of said Board. [*As amended by Section* 27 *of the Act of* 1861.

Notice to tax payers.

SEC. 9. The Common Council, after the expiration of said two weeks, or extended period in which the Board of Review are to sit, as above provided, for reviewing their assessment rolls, shall, at its next regular session, proceed to consider said assessment rolls, and any person aggrieved by the assessment of his property, and the decision of such Board of

Appeal to Common Council.

Review thereon, may appeal to the Common Council at said regular session. Every appeal shall be in writing, and shall state specially the grounds of the appeal, and the matter complained of, and no other matter shall be considered by the Council. While acting upon said assessment rolls, or appeals, any member of said Board may meet with the Common Council, and make such explanations as they may deem requisite in any case.

Common Council to hear appeals summarily.

SEC. 10. The Common Council shall hear and determine all appeals in a summary manner, and correct any errors which they may discover in the assessment rolls, and may place thereon the names of any persons and the descriptions of any property not already assessed, and assess the same, and may increase or diminish any assessment, as they may see fit: *Provided*, That they shall not increase any assessment of property without giving a reasonable opportunity to the persons owning or having charge of the same, if known, to appear and object thereto.

Proviso.

Hearing appeals may be continued.

SEC. 11. The Common Council may continue the consideration of said assessment rolls, and the hearing of said appeals, from session to session, for a period not exceeding sixteen days after the time when they are to be first considered as above provided, and on or before the expiration of said period of sixteen days, they shall be fully and finally confirmed by the Common Council, and shall remain as the basis of all taxes to be levied and collected in the city of Detroit, according to property valuation until another assessment shall have been made and confirmed, as above provided for.

Assessor to extend taxes upon rolls.

SEC. 12. After the assessment rolls shall have been fully and finally confirmed, as provided in the preceding section, it shall be the duty of the Assessor to cause the amount of all taxes, in dollars and cents, authorized to be assessed and collected in each year, to be rateably assessed to each person named, or lots described, upon and according to the aggregate valuation such person or lots shall have been assessed in said assessment rolls or books, prepared for that purpose, to be known as the tax rolls for each ward, in separate columns, showing the amount of highway, sewer, school, and city taxes assessed to each person or lots in each year; and when said tax rolls shall have been completed, the Assessor shall deliver the same to the Controller, who shall cause the same to be delivered to the Receiver of Taxes, and take his receipt therefor, and charge him therewith. Upon the receipt of the tax rolls by the Receiver of Taxes, as hereinbefore provided, the taxes therein stated shall become due and payable, and the Receiver of Taxes shall forthwith, upon the reception of said tax rolls, give six days' notice, by publication in two or more daily papers published in said city, and by posting the same in at least six public places in each ward, which notice shall be a sufficient demand for the payment of all taxes on said rolls; that the general tax rolls have been deposited with him, and that payment of the taxes therein specified may be made to him, at any time before the thirtieth day of December thereafter; that no addition will be made to taxes paid before the first day of August, but that an addition of one per cent. of every unpaid tax will be made thereto on that day, and a like addition of one per cent. every thirtieth day thereafter, until such addition shall amount to six per cent. of such tax. Upon the receipt of any tax, the Receiver shall mark the same paid upon the proper roll, and give a receipt therefor. On the first day of January, next following the time when any tax shall become due and payable, the Receiver shall add to every such tax six per cent. of the amount thereof, as stated in the roll, and the amount of the tax, and of such additions as are hereinbefore specified, shall thenceforth be the unpaid tax, and shall bear interest from that day, at the rate of twelve per cent. per annum, until paid, except as is herein otherwise provided. On or before the fifteenth day of January, the Receiver shall make, in duplicate, a roll of the unpaid taxes of each ward; such roll shall be a substantial

Duty of Controller.

Duty of Receiver.

Notice by.

Per centage added.

transcript of such portions of the original tax rolls as relate to the unpaid taxes, and shall exhibit the original, and in the last column, the augmented amount of every such tax. Immediately after completing such roll, he shall cause a

Notice.

notice to be published in five successive numbers of at least two daily newspapers published in said city, stating that said roll of unpaid taxes has been made, and that it will remain in his office, where such taxes may be paid, until the first day of February following, after which the property against which such taxes are assessed, shall be advertised and sold, as hereinafter provided. But the Receiver of Taxes, with the advice and consent of the Controller, on or after the first day of August in each year, may cause to be made out, copies of any taxes remaining due and unpaid on said tax or assessment rolls for each ward, and which are assessed wholly or partly against any property or value other than real estate, together with such per centage as shall have been fixed by the Common Council as compensation for the collection of such taxes or assessments, and to be stated in such rolls, and warrants may be issued and annexed to each such tax or assessment roll, signed by the Controller, and under the corporate seal of the corpo-

Warrants to collectors.

ration, directed to the proper ward Collector, or Collector

Return.

of the city, as the case may be, and made returnable upon such day as shall have been designated by the Common

Duty of collectors.

Council, commanding them to collect from the persons named in their respective assessment rolls, the assessment or taxes therein specified and set forth as due from such persons, and for such purpose, if necessary, to levy upon and sell the personal property of such person, occupant, or lessee, refusing or neglecting to pay the same, wherever the same may be found, within the limits of said city, and to pay over and account for the taxes or assessments thus collected, according to law. The Receiver of Taxes shall charge the amount of any such tax or assessment rolls, upon which warrants may be issued, to the Collectors of the proper ward, or of the city, as the case may be, and shall take a receipt therefor. Warrants for the collection of taxes and assessments, may be renewed and extended, from time to time, by the Common Council; but the time for the payment of any general tax shall not be extended beyond the first day of January following the time when such tax shall have become due and payable. It shall be the duty of the Assessor to make copies of said rolls, as finally confirmed by the Common Council, upon which he shall rateably assess the county and State taxes, as provided by the general laws of the State. [*As amended by Section* 28 *of the Act of* 1861.

Warrants may be renewed.

Duty of Assessor as to State and county taxes.

SEC. 13. By virtue of said warrants, the several Collectors, to whom they may be respectively directed, shall have power to levy upon the personal property of persons from whom taxes may be due, or the personal property of the occupant or lessee of any land or lot on which the tax may have been assessed, wherever the same may be found, within the limits of said city, and shall sell the same in the same manner, and with the same duties and powers of proceeding, as now or hereafter may be provided by the laws of this State, for the collection of State and county taxes, by Township Treasurers or Collectors; and all moneys thus collected, shall be paid over to the Receiver of Taxes, and all moneys received by the Receiver of Taxes, shall be paid over to the Treasurer of said city, as shall be prescribed by the Common Council. [*As amended by Section* 29 *of the Act of* 1861.

Powers of collectors.

Collectors to account to Receiver and Receiver to Treasurer.

SEC. 14. Every assessment or tax lawfully levied or imposed by the authority of the Common Council, on any lands, tenements, hereditaments, or premises whatsoever, in said city, shall be and remain a lien on such lands, tenements, hereditaments, or premises, from and after the time such taxes shall become due and payable as aforesaid; and the owner or occupants of, or parties in interest in said real estate, shall be liable to pay every such tax or assessment, and if there be default in paying the same, or any

Taxes a lien on property.

Delinquent taxes.

part thereof, or if such person or persons be non-resident of said city, it shall be lawful for said Common Council to cause a notice to be published in the daily newspaper, published by the printer for the city, once a week, for four successive weeks, and posted in three or more public places in each ward, requiring the owners or occupants of, or parties in interest in such lands, tenements, hereditaments, or premises, to pay such assessment or tax, and that if default be made in making such payment, such real estate will be sold at public auction, at a day and place to be specified in said notice, for the lowest term of years at which any person shall offer to take the same, in consideration of advancing and paying such assessment or tax, with the costs or charges in the premises. [*As amended by Section* 30 *of the Act of* 1861.

Notice.

Sale at auction.

Sale of real estate for taxes for term of years.

SEC. 15. If the owners or occupants of, or parties in interest in such real estate, do not pay such assessment or taxes, with the costs and charges, within the period above prescribed for the publication of said notice, then the said Common Council shall have power, without any further notice, to cause such real estate to be sold at public auction for the lowest term of years at which any person shall offer to take the same, in consideration of advancing such assessment or tax, with the costs and charges, and to direct the execution of a proper certificate of such sale to the purchaser thereof; and if such real estate shall not be redeemed within one year after such sale thereof, as herein after provided, the Controller shall, in the name of and for the City of Detroit, execute and deliver to such purchaser or his assignee, a proper deed for the conveyance of such real estate, for the term for which the same was sold, which deed shall in all courts be *prima facie* evidence of the regularity of all the proceedings under which the sale was made, and said deed was executed, up to the date of the deed; and any person who shall under such deed enter into any such real estate, and erect or place any building or building materials thereon,

Redemption.

Controller to execute deed of real estate for term of years.

Deed *prima facie* evidence of regularity of proceedings.

shall have the right at any time within three months after the expiration of said term, or in case he shall be ousted before the expiration of such term by any person claiming adversely to said deed, then within three months after trial, judgment of ouster or ejectment, to remove such building or building materials from said real estate.

Purchaser may erect buildings on premises sold and may remove the same within three months after expiration of term.

SEC. 16. When any lands, tenements and hereditaments shall be sold according to the foregoing provisions for the payment of any assessment or tax, as aforesaid, if the owners or occupants of or parties in interest in the same shall within one year after such sale deposit with the Treasurer of said city, for the use of the purchaser, the full amount of the assessment or tax for which such real estate was sold, and such interest as the Common Council shall prescribe, as hereinafter authorized, together with the amount of the costs and charges, then the term for which such real estate was sold shall cease and be determined at the time of making such deposit, subject, however, to the right of the purchaser, his heirs, executors, administrators, or assigns, to remove any building or building materials as hereinbefore provided.

Redemption.

SEC. 17. Any person in possession of any real estate at the time any tax is to be collected, shall be liable to pay the tax imposed thereon, and in case any other person, by agreement or otherwise, ought to pay such tax or any part thereof, the person in possession who shall pay the same, may recover the amount paid from the person who ought to have paid the same, in an action of assumpsit, as for moneys paid out and expended for his use and benefit.

Taxes paid may be recovered of person who ought to pay the same in action of assumpsit.

SEC. 18. The Common Council shall have power to charge interest at a rate not exceeding twenty-five per cent. per annum, from the time of sale, on the amount of any assessment or tax, for the non-payment of which any lands, tenements or hereditaments may be sold, and upon the amount to be paid upon the redemption of any such real estate and premises so sold. [*As amended by Section* 31 *of the Act of* 1861.

Interest on redemption.

Right to remove buildings.

SEC. 19. Any person who shall at such sale purchase for a term of years any lots, grounds or wharves, shall have the right to remove any building or building materials erected or deposited by or belonging to him, and situated on said lots, grounds or wharves, at any time within three months after the expiration of the term or time for which the same were sold.

Controller or Mayor may execute conveyances.

SEC. 20. The Controller, or in his absence the Mayor, may execute, in the name of the corporation, and under its corporate seal, proper conveyances or certificates of sale of all lands, tenements, or hereditaments sold for assessments or taxes, which, when duly acknowledged and attested by the City Clerk, may be recorded as other conveyances of land under the laws of this State.

Controller to bid where no one offers to bid.

SEC. 21. It shall be the duty of the Controller, to bid in for the corporation, at any sale of real estate for assessments or taxes, every lot of land or premises for which no person shall offer to bid; and if any purchaser shall refuse or neglect to pay the sum or sums bid by him, within the time and under the regulations prescribed by the Common Council, such bid shall enure to the use and benefit of the corporation, if the Common Council so elect. Upon all such bids by the Controller, and all bids as aforesaid, to the use and benefit of the corporation, conveyances and certificates of sale may be executed by the Controller to the corporation, acknowledged and attested by the City Clerk, and recorded in the same manner as provided in other cases of sale for assessment or taxes. But in all cases of sales for special assessments, the property so bid in for the corporation, may, at the option of the Common Council, be held in trust for the person or contractor in whose behalf such assessment shall have been made, or his assignee, or upon payment to such person or contractor of the amount for which such property shall have been bid in, the city may, as in case of the general tax, become the owner of the tax title or lease thus obtained, and may dispose

Certificates of sale.

Sales for special assessments.

of the same as if obtained under a like sale for any general tax. [*As amended by Section* 32 *of the Act of* 1861.

Conveyance to be *prima facie* evidence.

SEC. 22. All conveyances, certificates of sale and leases of any lands, tenements or hereditaments, executed by the corporation or any of its officers by virtue of this act, shall be taken and received in all courts and proceedings as *prima facie* evidence of the regularity of the proceedings on which such conveyances, certificates of sale, lease, or any title claimed thereby, are founded.

Assessment rolls for sewers, sidewalks and paving.

SEC. 23. Assessment rolls to defray the expense of constructing lateral sewers, side and crosswalks, paving, grading, macadamizing, graveling or otherwise improving streets, lanes or alleys, or for defraying the expense of any local improvements properly payable from the proceeds of special assessment, shall be placed in the hands of the Receiver of taxes, for payment as may be provided by ordinance or resolution of the Common Council for the space of thirty days, after which warrants for the collection of the same may be issued, and such proceedings for the collection thereof be had as are or shall be prescribed by law, or by any ordinance or resolution of the Common Council, and sales of any real or personal estate for any unpaid assessments shall be made in like manner and with like effect, as in case of sales for non-payment of the general tax. [*As amended by Section* 33 *of the Act of* 1861.

Warrants.

# CHAPTER X.

## FIRE DEPARTMENT.



Common Council to buy engines, etc.

SECTION 1. The Common Council shall procure fire engines, hose, hooks, ladders and other apparatus and implements used for the extinguishment of fires, for each fire company, pay the expenses of keeping the same in necessary repair, have charge and control of the same, and provide fit and secure engine houses and other places for keeping and preserving the same, and purchase any real estate for the erection of engine houses.

To organize fire companies.

SEC. 2. The Common Council shall have power to organize engine, hook, hose, ladder, ax and other fire companies, for the prevention and extinguishment of fires, and to dissolve or disband the same; to appoint a competent number of able inhabitants of the City of Detroit firemen, to take the care and management of engines, hose, ladders, and other apparatus and implements used and provided for the prevention and extinguishment of fires; to prescribe the duties and powers of firemen and fire companies, make rules and regulations for their government, impose reasonable fines, penalties and forfeitures upon them for a violation of the same, and to remove them for incapacity, neglect of duty or misconduct.

SEC. 3. There shall be a Chief Engineer and two or more Assistant Engineers, who shall be appointed by the firemen with the consent and confirmation of the Common Council, and whose powers and duties shall be prescribed by said Council. Chief Engineer and Assistants.

SEC. 4. The Mayor, members of the Common Council, Marshal and Deputy Marshals, by virtue of their offices, shall be Fire Wardens, and the Common Council may annually appoint one or more resident electors of each ward, Fire Wardens thereof, who shall hold office until removed, or their successors be appointed and qualified. Fire Wardens.

SEC. 5. Each fire company shall have power to appoint its own officers, make by-laws and regulations for its good government, not inconsistent with this act or the ordinances and regulations of the Common Council, and may impose and collect such fines for the non-attendance or neglect of duty of any of its members, as may be prescribed by the by-laws or regulations of said company, and it shall be the duty of each fire company, subject to the control and regulations of the Common Council, to take the care and management of the fire engine, hose, hook, ladder and other fire apparatus and implements of such company, to keep the same in good and perfect repair, and upon any fire alarm or breaking out of any fire within said city, it shall be the duty of each member of a fire company forthwith to repair to the engine house of such company and thence proceed, without delay, with its engine, hose or other fire apparatus and implements, to the place of such fire, and there use the same, and otherwise labor for the extinguishment of such fire, under the direction of the Chief Engineer or other officers present, who may be empowered by the Common Council to give orders and directions at a fire in relation to the extinguishment thereof. Powers and duties of fire companies and firemen.

SEC. 6. It shall also be the duty of each fire company to assemble once in each month, or as often as may be directed by the Common Council, for the purpose of working and Meetings of companies.

examining its engine, hose or other fire apparatus and implements, and putting and keeping them in perfect order and repair.

Powers and duties of Fire Wardens.

SEC. 7. The Fire Wardens appointed for the several wards shall have power, at all reasonable times, and it shall be their duty to enter into and examine all the dwelling-houses, out-houses, lots and yards in their respective wards; to ascertain how ashes are kept; to direct full obedience to all ordinances of the Common Council, relating to the prevention of fires, and to report to the Common Council all infractions thereof; and the Mayor, members of the Common Council, Marshal and Deputy Marshals, acting as Fire Wardens, shall have the same powers and perform the same duties within the limits of said city which the appointed Fire Wardens may have and perform within the limits of their respective wards.

Exemption of firemen.

SEC. 8. Every person, while serving as fireman, or who shall have served as fireman in said city for a term of five years, shall be exempted from serving as a juror and from doing militia duty, except in case of war, invasion or insurrection. A certificate of such service, under the seal of the corporation, signed by the Mayor and Clerk of the city, or as prescribed in the act incorporating "The Fire Department of the City of Detroit," approved February 14th, 1840, shall be, in all courts and places, evidence of such exemption. The Engineers, Assistant Engineers, Fire Wardens appointed for the several wards, and members of engine, hook, hose, ladder and other fire companies lawfully organized, shall be deemed firemen of said city within the meaning of this section.

Powers of certain officers at fires.

SEC. 9. The Mayor, any member of the Common Council, Engineer or Fire Warden, may order all able-bodied persons present at a fire to assist and labor in the extinguishment thereof and in the preservation of property, and may also order all persons present at a fire, not belonging to the Fire Department or not lawfully employed in its service or in the preservation and custody of property, to remove from the vicinity of such fire all property exposed by reason thereof.

SEC. 10. Whenever any person shall refuse to obey any lawful order of the Mayor, any member of the Common Council, Engineer, or Fire Warden at any fire, it shall be lawful for the officer giving such order, to arrest or to direct orally the Marshal, any Deputy Marshal, Constable, Policeman or any citizen to arrest such person and confine him temporarily, until such fire be extinguished; and such officers or any of them may arrest or direct the arrest and temporary confinement of any person at such fire who shall be intoxicated or disorderly.

Power of officer at fire to arrest for disobedience of order.

SEC. 11. Upon the breaking out of any fire within said city, the Marshal, Deputy Marshals, Constables and appointed Fire Wardens shall immediately repair to the place of such fire with their staves, and aid and assist in extinguishing such fire, and in removing, securing, preserving and preventing from being stolen, any goods or other property exposed by reason of such fire, and shall in all respects be obedient to the lawful orders of the Mayor, any member of the Common Council or Engineer present.

Duties of officers upon breaking out of fires.

SEC. 12. Engine, hose, hook, ladder and other fire companies, now organized within the City of Detroit, shall be continued in their organization until dissolved or disbanded, and the present firemen, fire engineers and fire wardens of said city are hereby continued in office until removed; but said companies, firemen, and fire engineers shall in all respects be governed by this act in respect to their powers, duties, liabilities, term and tenure of office, and by the ordinances, rules and regulations of the Common Council made pursuant to the provisions of this act.

Present fire companies continued until dissolved or disbanded.

Sec. 13. (*Note A.*) The Common Council may, on the nomination of the Mayor, appoint a Fire Marshal, whose duty it shall be to investigate the cause and origin of all fires which shall happen within the city, and for that purpose he shall have power to administer oaths, and examine

Fire Marshal.

Powers.

witnesses touching such investigations. He shall have power to issue subpoenas requiring the attendance of witnesses. Disobedience to such subpoenas shall render the witness liable to the same penalties as for like disobedience in courts of record.

Testimony taken on investigation.

SEC. 14. (*Note A.*) The testimony taken on such investigation shall be reduced to writing, and signed by the witness, when the Marshal shall proceed to determine, from the circumstances proved before him, the true cause and origin of the fire, and reduce the same to writing, under his hand, and report the same, together with the testimony, to the Common Council.

Cause of fires.

To make complaints.

SEC. 15. (*Note A.*) If in the course of such investigation, or at the close thereof, he shall have good reason to believe that any person or persons willfully set, or caused such fire to be set, he shall forthwith make complaint before some magistrate having jurisdiction in such cases, and cause the parties complained of to be apprehended.

Term of.

SEC. 16. (*Note A.*) The term of the office of Fire Marshal shall be one year from the second Tuesday of January in each year, and until a successor shall be appointed and enter upon the duties of the office. He shall perform such other duties as the Common Council shall direct. He shall be subject to removal in the same manner provided for the removal of other officers appointed by the Common Council. The person first appointed shall hold the office until the second Tuesday in January, 1862, subject to removal as aforesaid.

How removed.

---

NOTE A.—Sections 13, 14, 15 and 16 were added to this chapter by sec. 34 of the act of 1861.

# CHAPTER XI.

## MISCELLANEOUS PROVISIONS.



SECTION 1. The corporation created by this act, shall pay and discharge all the debts, obligations, contracts, and liabilities of "The Mayor, Recorder, Aldermen, and Freemen of the City of Detroit," and suits may be brought and prosecuted thereon, against said corporation, in law or equity, to the same effect as they could be brought and prosecuted against "The Mayor, Recorder, Aldermen, and Freemen of the City of Detroit," if this act had not been passed.

New corporation to pay debts of old.

SEC. 2. All property, real, personal, and mixed, and rights of property, in law or in equity, and all debts, fines, penalties, forfeitures, rights, and causes of action, and all rights and powers not inconsistent with the provisions of this act, which belong, have accrued, or may accrue to "The Mayor, Recorder, Aldermen, and Freemen of the City of Detroit," or to the inhabitants of the City of Detroit, in their corporate capacity, shall be, and the same are hereby declared to be fully and absolutely vested in the corporation created by this act, to be held subject to the provisions hereof, and may be prosecuted for, and recovered or claimed, asserted and maintained by said corporation, in its own name, or in any other lawful manner.

Rights vested in corporation under this act.

Actions pending continued.

SEC. 3. All writs, prosecutions, actions, and causes of action, now in suit, and instituted or commenced, by or against "The Mayor, Recorder, Aldermen, and Freemen of the City of Detroit," shall continue, and may be prosecuted to the end thereof, to the same effect as if this act had not been passed.

Mayor's court continued until Recorder's court organized.

SEC. 4. The Mayor's Court, of the City of Detroit, except as herein otherwise provided, shall continue, with its powers and jurisdiction, as if this act had not been passed, until the organization of the Recorder's Court, under this act, and from and after such organization, its powers and jurisdiction shall cease.

Removal of records, etc., to Recorder's court.

SEC. 5. On the organization of the Recorder's Court, all books, records, recognizances, and papers, filed in or pertaining to the Mayor's Court of the City of Detroit, and all proceedings, commenced or cognizable therein, shall be removed and transferred to, or commenced in said Recorder's Court, and proceeded with in conformity with its powers and jurisdiction, to the same effect as if this act had not been passed.

Causes of action continued.

SEC. 6. All causes of action, rights, and liabilities of individuals of the State, and of bodies corporate, shall continue and remain, as if this act had not been passed, except of "The Mayor, Recorder, Aldermen, and Freemen of the City of Detroit," whose act of incorporation is hereby repealed.

Certain acts not invalidated.

SEC. 7. This act shall not invalidate any legal act done by "The Mayor, Recorder, Aldermen, and Freemen of the City of Detroit," or by the Common Council, or any officer of said city, now or heretofore in office.

Ordinances to remain in force.

SEC. 8. All ordinances, by-laws, regulations, resolutions, and rules of the Common Council of the City of Detroit, now in force, and not inconsistent with this act, shall remain in force until altered, amended, or repealed by the Common Council, under this act, and after the same shall take effect.

SEC. 9. No person shall be an incompetent judge, justice of the peace, or other officer, witness, or juror, by reason of his being an inhabitant or freeholder in the City of Detroit, in any prosecution or proceeding in the Recorder's Court, in any action or proceeding in which the corporation shall be a party in interest, or in any judicial or other proceeding. Inhabitants of Detroit not to be incompetent as jurors, etc.

SEC. 10. The certificate of the Clerk, required by this act, specifying the day on which he may have presented any ordinance, resolution, or proceeding to the Mayor, for his approval or disapproval, or a copy thereof, certified by such Clerk, under the seal of the corporation, shall, in all courts, places, and proceedings, be conclusive evidence of the facts therein stated. Clerk's certificate to be conclusive evidence.

SEC. 11. The record of any ordinance enacted, and of the time of its first publication, made by the Clerk, as required in this act, or a copy thereof, certified by such Clerk, under the seal of the corporation, shall be presumptive evidence in all courts, places, and proceedings, of the due passage of such ordinance, of its having been duly published, and of the time of its first publication. Copies of all other records and papers, duly filed in and pertaining to the office of the Clerk, certified by him, under the seal of the corporation, shall be evidence in all courts and places, to the same effect as the originals would be, if produced. Records or certified copies of records to be presumptive evidence.

SEC. 12. Proof of the requisite publication of any ordinance, resolution, or other proceeding, required to be published in any newspaper, by the affidavit of a printer or publisher thereof, taken before any officer authorized to administer oaths and take affidavits, and duly filed with the Clerk of the city, or any other competent proof, shall, in all courts and places, be conclusive evidence of the legal publication of such ordinance, resolution, or other proceeding. Proof of publication of ordinances, etc.

SEC. 13. All ordinances and by-laws of the Common Council, printed and published by their authority, shall, in all courts, places, and proceedings, be received without further proof as *prima facie* evidence thereof, and of their legal enactment and publication.

Perjury. SEC. 14. Any person required to take any oath or affirmation, or to make any affidavit or statement, under oath or affirmation, under any provision of this act, who shall, under such oath or affirmation, in any such statement or affidavit, or otherwise, willfully swear falsely as to any material matter, shall be guilty of perjury, and may be prosecuted therefor, and, on conviction, punished, as in the case of perjury under the general laws of this State.

Public act. SEC. 15. This act shall be deemed a public act, and shall be construed benignly and favorably for any beneficial purpose therein intended.

This act may be amended. SEC. 16. This act may at any time be altered or amended by the Legislature of this State.

---

# CHAPTER XII.

## ACTS CONTINUED AND REPEALED.

SECTION 1. The following acts and part of acts, being now in force, shall be continued, subject to this act, viz.:

The act entitled "An Act to incorporate the Fire Department of the City of Detroit," approved February 14th, 1840;

The act entitled "An Act to amend the laws relative to supplying the City of Detroit with pure and wholesome water, and to provide for the completion and management of the Detroit Water Works," approved February 14th, 1853;

The act entitled "An Act to authorize the Water Commissioners of the City of Detroit to loan money for the purpose of extending and improving the Water Works of said city," approved February 6th, 1855;

All acts and parts of acts relating to schools in the City of Detroit;

The act entitled "An Act amending an act relative to the registry of certain deeds, approved March 9th, 1844," approved May 7th, 1846;

The act entitled "An Act relative to conveyances in the City of Detroit," approved April 1st, 1850;

The act entitled "An Act to incorporate the City of Detroit Gas Company," approved March 14th, 1849, and all acts amendatory thereof.

Sections eight, nine, ten, eleven, and twelve, of chapter one hundred and three of the Revised Statutes of 1846, relating to the selection and return of jurors from said city, to serve in the Circuit Court for the County of Wayne;

Section forty-nine, of chapter thirty-five, of the Revised Statutes of 1846, relating to Boards of Health in cities and villages;

The act entitled "An Act to establish a Police Court in the City of Detroit," approved April 2d, 1850, and all acts and parts of acts amendatory thereof;

The act entitled "An Act to provide for draining certain low lands in the vicinity of Detroit," approved March 29th, 1849;

SEC. 2. The following acts and parts of acts are hereby repealed, viz.:

The act of the Legislative Council of the Territory of Michigan, granting a charter of incorporation to "The Mayor, Recorder, Aldermen, and Freemen of the City of Detroit," and entitled "An Act relative to the City of Detroit," approved April 4th, 1827, and all acts and parts of acts amending or altering said act or charter, and not hereby continued; and all other acts and parts of acts relating to the City of Detroit, and not hereby continued, the subjects whereof are revised and re-enacted, in this act, or which are repugnant to or inconsistent with the provisions of this act.

---

# CHAPTER XIII.

*(Note A.)*

## POLICE DEPARTMENT.



Police Commissioners; how appointed; terms of office; powers.

SECTION 1. The Mayor and two other persons, who shall be appointed by the Common Council, and who shall hold office during the pleasure of the Common Council, shall constitute a Board of Police Commissioners for the City of Detroit. Such board, or a majority of them, shall have full power to try and determine all complaints against the Chief of Police, or any Policeman, or Watchman of the city, and to remove them, or any of them, summarily, on conviction, for insubordination, neglect of duty, or violation of any of the ordinances, or the rules and regulations made, or hereafter

---

NOTE A.—New chapter; see section 35 of the act of 1861.

to be made for the government of the police department of the City of Detroit. The City Clerk shall be the Clerk of said Board, and shall keep its records. Said Commissioners shall receive no compensation. Clerk of.

SEC. 2. Such Board, when convened for the purposes mentioned in the preceding section, shall be vested with full power to subpœna witnesses, issue warrants to compel the attendance of witnesses, administer oaths, take and record testimony, and to do such other acts as may lawfully be done by any court, for the purpose mentioned in section one of this chapter. Power to subpœna witnesses on investigation.

SEC. 3. The Mayor or Chief of Police may suspend any Policeman from his office, on charge of misconduct, until the trial and decision of the Board of Police Commissioners shall be had. Notice in writing, that charges or accusations are made, or are to be presented before the Board of Police Commissioners, shall be given to such member or members of the police department as are accused of official misconduct, neglect of duty, or other offenses to be tried by said Board, at least twenty-four hours before such trial shall be had. The Board may continue the suspension, remove the accused from office, or restore him to duty. Who may suspend policemen. Trial of. Notice. Penalty.

SEC. 4. The Chief of Police shall be appointed by the Common Council, on the nomination of the Board of Police Commissioners, and shall hold his office at the pleasure of the Council. He shall, under said Board, be the chief executive of the police department. He shall have the same power conferred upon Policemen by this act, and shall possess all the powers of the Police Justice of the City of Detroit, to entertain complaints for criminal offenses, and to issue warrants for the arrest of persons charged with such offenses, but such warrants shall be made returnable before the Police Justice of the city, at his office. He shall also have power to commit persons charged with criminal offenses, until examination shall be had before the Police Justice. He shall obey, and cause the police department to Chief of Police; how appointed. Power of. Duty of obey the rules and regulations prescribed by the ordinances of the Common Council, and the rules and regulations prescribed by the Board of Police Commissioners, and shall perform such other duties as shall, from time to time, be prescribed by the Common Council.

Police station.

SEC. 5. The Common Council shall provide suitable accommodation for the Police, to be designated "The Police Station."

Board power to appoint watchmen.

SEC. 6. The Board of Police Commissioners shall have power to appoint Watchmen, without compensation, who shall possess the same powers, as conservators of the peace, which township constables possess, under the general laws of the State.

Additional policemen; how appointed.

SEC. 7. The Common Council, on the nomination of the Board of Police Commissioners, when, in their opinion, it is necessary for the preservation of the peace and good order of the city, may appoint additional temporary Policemen, but such appointment shall not continue beyond forty-eight hours, unless otherwise ordered by the Common Council.

Board power to make rules and regulations.

SEC. 8. The Board of Police Commissioners shall have power, and it shall be their duty, from time to time, to prescribe the duties, and make such rules and regulations for the management and government of the police department, as they shall think proper, not inconsistent with the provisions of this chapter, and the ordinances of the Common Council.

Power to arrest without warrant.

SEC. 9. Whenever any person or persons shall violate any of the ordinances of the city, relative to breaches of the peace, any member of the police department may, under general regulations, to be prescribed by the Board of Police Commissioners, and without process, arrest such person or persons, and take them before the Chief of Police, and make complaint, who is empowered to hold to bail or commit such person or persons, to appear before the Police Court, or the Recorder's Court.

SEC. 10. The Police Justice of the City of Detroit shall have jurisdiction to hear and determine such offenses for any violations of the city ordinances, as the Common Council shall, by ordinance, prescribe. All fines so imposed and collected by said Police Justice, shall be paid into the city treasury immediately after their collection.

Council may give Police Justice jurisdiction of offenses against ordinances.

SEC. 11. It shall be the duty of the Police Justice to attend the police station house at such times as shall be prescribed by the Common Council; he shall summarily examine into the case of every person confined in said station house, and if he adjudge any person guilty of vagrancy, disorderly conduct, or any violation of the city ordinances, relative to breaches of the peace, he may convict such person or persons thereof, and commit him or her to the Wayne County jail, or house of correction, for not more than six months, and impose a fine not exceeding fifty dollars, and in default of the immediate payment thereof, to commit such person or persons to the Wayne County jail, or to the house of correction, for a term not exceeding six months, or until such fine be paid. All fines imposed, shall be paid into the city treasury. He shall detain, for examination, all persons charged with offenses against the laws of the State, and not punishable under the ordinances of the city, as aforesaid, for examination before the Police Court: *Provided*, The Common Council, at any regular meeting thereof, may designate any Justice of the Peace of the City of Detroit, who shall have the power to perform the duties prescribed by this section; but in case of the death, absence from the city, sickness, or other disability, the Police Justice shall perform said duties; said Police Justice, or Justice of the Peace, shall receive such compensation for performing the duties required by this and the foregoing section, as the Common Council shall prescribe, and the Police Justice, and the Justice of the Peace, so designated, shall have exclusive jurisdiction in all cases properly cognizable by the Police Justice.

Duty of Police Justice.

To attend station houses.

Fines; to whom paid.

Proviso.

Council to designate Justice of the Peace to act in case of sickness, etc. of Police Justice.

SEC. 12. The Common Council shall designate, on the second Tuesday of January in each year, or at some regular meeting thereof, one of the Justices of the Peace elected in said city, to act as Police Justice, in case of the death, sickness, absence, or other disability of the Police Justice; and the Justice so designated, shall, during such disability, or the continuance of any vacancy in the office of Police Justice, have exclusive jurisdiction of all cases properly cognizable in the Police Court of said city, and shall have, and may exercise the same powers as may be exercised by the Police Justice of said city; and the Justice so exercising the duties of Police Justice, shall be paid such compensation as the Common Council shall direct—such compensation to be drawn from the fund applicable to the payment of the Police Justice. Such designation may be revoked by the Common Council, upon the recommendation of the Mayor, and another Justice designated. The Justice first designated, under the above provision, shall hold his office until the second Tuesday of January, eighteen hundred and sixty-two. The Police Justice of said city may be removed in the same manner and for the same causes as Justices of the Peace.

Power of Justice of the Peace.

Compensation.

How appointment revoked.

How Police Justice removed.

Council may offer rewards.

SEC. 13. The Common Council shall have power, by a vote of two-thirds of all the Aldermen elected, to authorize the Board of Police Commissioners to offer a reward for the detection and apprehension of any offender against the city ordinances, or of the perpetrator of any high crime or misdemeanor, committed within the city, to be paid on the conviction of such offender or criminal.

---

NOTE.—The Act of 1861 was ordered to take effect immediately.

# ACTS

OF THE

# LEGISLATURE RELATING TO THE CITY.

---

## AN ACT to Enlarge the Corporate Limits of the City of Detroit.

[*Approved February 12th*, 1857.]

---

SECTION 1. *The People of the State of Michigan enact*, That from and after the passage of this act the following district of country shall constitute the City of Detroit, to wit: Beginning at the national boundary line in Detroit River on the continuation of the dividing line between private claims numbered 21 and 78, as confirmed by the Board of Land Commissioners of the United States; thence northerly along said dividing line to the southerly line of the Detroit, Monroe and Toledo Railroad; thence north-easterly along said line to the present western boundary of the City of Detroit; thence northerly along said boundary to the north-western corner of said city; thence eastwardly along the present northerly boundary line of said city to the north-east corner of private claim number 14, known as the St. Aubin farm; thence southerly along the line between said claim number 14 and private claim number 91, to a point where the northerly line of Leland street, when extended in a right line eastwardly from the said city, would intersect the line between said claims; thence eastwardly at right angles with the side lines of said claims to the easterly line of private claims number 9 **Boundaries.**

and 454; thence southerly along the line between private claims number 9 and 454 and private claims number 11 and 453, being between the farms known as the McDougal and Chapoton farms, to the northerly line of the Fort Gratiot turnpike; thence north-easterly along said northerly line of said turnpike to the easterly line of private claim number 15; thence southerly along the easterly line of said claim number 15 to said national boundary line; thence westwardly along said national boundary to the place of beginning.

Wards.

SEC. 2. So much of the above described district as lies below, or westward, of the present corporate limits of said city, shall constitute one ward, to be known and designated as the ninth ward of said city; and so much of said district as lies above, or eastward, of the present corporate limits of said city, shall constitute one ward, to be known and designated as the tenth ward of said city. And from and after the time above fixed for the taking effect of this act, the said district hereby annexed to said city shall be subject to all laws, ordinances and regulations which shall at any time be in force over the remainder of said city, and shall cease to be subject to the regulations or government of any other township: *Provided*, That the Common Council of the City of Detroit may at any time alter or divide the said wards in the manner provided by the Charter of said city for the regulation or alteration of the present wards thereof.

Proviso.

Election of Aldermen.

SEC. 3. There shall be elected, at the next ensuing charter election to be held in said city, two persons in each of said wards to serve as Aldermen, one in each ward to serve one year, and one in each ward to serve for two years, and the time of service for which each Alderman is elected shall be designated on the ballots cast for such officers respectively; and such other ward officers shall be elected at such election, as are provided for the other wards of said city, and the terms of office of all such Aldermen and officers shall correspond with those of similar Aldermen and officers in such other wards.

Other ward officers.

SEC. 4. The Common Council of the City of Detroit may at any time before said charter election appoint the places for holding the same in the said ninth and tenth wards, and said election shall be conducted in like manner with those in the other wards of said city, except that, at eight o'clock in the forenoon of the day for holding said charter election, the electors of said wards present at the place of holding the polls shall elect, *viva voce*, three of their own number to act as inspectors of said election, who shall be sworn rightfully to discharge the duties of such inspectors, (which oath either of them may administer to the others,) and who shall be the legal inspectors of said election, and said inspectors in each ward may appoint one or more electors of each of said wards to act as constables at and about the polls of such wards during said election day.

Place of holding charter election in ninth and tenth wards may be appointed by Council.

Mode of conducting election therein.

SEC. 5. The Common Council may appoint any persons to fill any office in either of said wards, which is provided for in the other wards of said city, (except that of Alderman,) and the officers so appointed shall continue to act, until their successors are elected at said charter election, and are duly qualified, and no longer.

Persons may be appointed to fill ward offices.

SEC. 6. This act shall take effect and be in force from and after its passage. [*Laws of* 1857, *p.* 209.]

To take immediate effect.

---

AN ACT to amend the laws relative to "Supplying the City of Detroit with Pure and Wholesome Water," and to provide for the Completion and Management of the Detroit Water Works.

SECTION 1. *The People of the State of Michigan enact*, That Shubael Conant, Henry Ledyard, Edmund A. Brush, William R. Noyes and James A. Van Dyke, be, and they are hereby, named and constituted as a "Board of Water Commissioners of the City of Detroit;" who and their successors in office, shall be known by the name and style of the "Board of Water Commissioners of the City of Detroit,"

Name and style.

Powers. and by that name shall have power to contract, sue and be sued, to purchase, hold and convey personal and real estate, Seal. to have a common seal, to alter and change the same at pleasure, to make by-laws and ordinances, and do all legal acts which may be necessary and proper to carry out the effect, intent and object of this Act.

Term of office. SEC. 2. The said Commissioners shall hold their offices respectively for the term of three, four, five, six and seven years, from the first Tuesday in May, of the year one thousand eight hundred and fifty-three. Said Commissioners shall, within sixty days after the passage of this act, decide by lot their respestive terms, which decision shall be notified by a written statement to the Common Council of said city, which shall be entered of record on the books of the said Common Council; and at their first regular meeting in the month of April, in the year one thousand eight hundred and fifty-six, and annually thereafter, the said Common Council shall elect and appoint a citizen of said city, being a qualified voter and a freeholder, as a Commissioner, who shall hold his office for five years from the first Tuesday in the May next following: *Provided*, That this section shall not be so construed as to disqualify any member of the said Board for Vacancy; how filled. re-appointment. And in case of the death or resignation, or removal from the city, of any of said Commissioners, the Common Council shall, as soon thereafter as possible, appoint to fill such vacancy, for the remainder of the term, some citizen of said city, being a qualified voter and a freeholder.

President and Secretary. SEC. 3. The said Commissioners shall choose one of their own number as President, who shall hold his office until the first Tuesday of May next ensuing the date of his election; they shall also appoint some suitable person as Secretary, who shall hold his office at the pleasure of the Board. And in case of the death, resignation, or removal from the city of the President, the said Commissioners shall have power to fill the vacancy so happening as in the first instance.

SEC. 4. The said Commissioners shall have power to loan, from time to time, upon the best terms they can make, after giving public notice by advertising in the city papers for sixty days, and in one paper in Boston and two in New York, for such time as they shall deem expedient, a sum of money not exceeding two hundred and fifty thousand dollars, upon the credit of said city of Detroit, and shall have authority to issue bonds pledging the faith and credit of said city for the payment of the principal and interest of said bonds, which bonds shall issue under the seal of said Board of Commissioners, and shall be signed by them, or a majority of them, and bearing interest not exceeding eight per cent. per annum. And it shall be the duty of said Commissioners to cause to be kept an accurate register of all bonds issued by them, showing the number, date and amount of each bond, and to whom the same was issued; and it shall also be their duty to cause to be furnished to the auditor of said city a copy of such register, as soon as the same is made, which shall be preserved by said Auditor, and copied into the records of said city.

Power to loan money on bonds.

Registry of bonds.

Copy furnished Auditor.

SEC. 5. It shall be the duty of said Commissioners to examine and consider all matters relative to supplying the city of Detroit with a sufficient quantity of pure and wholesome water, to be taken from the Detroit River, or such other source as may be deemed expedient, for the use of its inhabitants.

Supply of water.

SEC. 6. Said Commissioners shall have power to employ superintendents, clerks, collectors, assessors, engineers, surveyors and such other persons as, in their opinion, may be necessary to enable them to perform their duties under this act, and to specify the duties of such persons so employed, and to fix their compensation: *Provided*, That in no case shall said Commissioners receive, directly or indirectly, any compensation for their own services.

Power to employ superintendents, etc.

Commissioners not to receive compensation.

SEC. 7. Said commisssoners shall have power, and it is hereby made their duty, as soon as may be, after the neces-

Power to purchase land, etc.

sary funds shall have been procured, as herein provided, to purchase such land and materials, and to construct such reservoirs, buildings, machinery and fixtures, as shall be deemed necessary or desirable to furnish a full supply of water for public and private use in said city.

Reservoirs, jets, hydrants, etc.

SEC. 8. Said Commissioners shall have power to construct reservoirs, jets and fire hydrants, at such localities in said city as they may deem expedient and necessary, and to lay pipes in and through all the alleys and streets of said city; and also to construct in such localities as they may deem expedient, not exceeding one to each block, hydrants for public use, and to keep the same in repair; and also, with the consent of the Common Council of said city, to construct fountains in the public squares, or such other public grounds of said city as they shall deem expedient.

Fountains in public squares.

Assessment of water rates.

SEC. 9. Said Commissioners shall, from time to time, cause to be assessed the water rate to be paid by the owner or occupant of each house or other building having or using water, upon such basis as they shall deem equitable; and such water rate shall become a continuing lien, until paid, upon such house or other building, and upon the lot or lots upon which such house or other building is situated.

Lien on premises.

Power to make by-laws.

SEC. 10. Said Commissioners shall have full power to make and enforce all necessary by-laws, rules and regulations for the collection of said water rates, either by the appointment of collectors to demand the same, requiring payment at the office, shutting off the water, or by a suit at law before any court of competent jurisdiction, or by sale of the lot or premises upon which such rates shall have become a lien: *Provided*, That such sales shall be conducted in the same manner, and shall have the same force, virtue and effect of sales of lots delinquent for city taxes: *And provided, further*, That the attempt to collect said rates by any process above mentioned shall not in any way invalidate the lien upon said lot or premises.

Sale of property for non-payment of water rates.

SEC. 11. The said Commissioners shall cause to be kept an accurate record of all proceedings, together with a list of all assessments for water rates, which shall be subject to inspection at all times. Record of proceedings.

SEC. 12. It shall be the duty of said Commissioners to make a report to the Common Council of said city annually, which report shall embrace a statement of the condition and operation of the works, a statement of the funds and securities of said Board, and all debts due and owing to and from said Board, together with an accurate account of their expenses; which statement shall be certified by said Commissioners, and shall be entered of record by the Clerk of said city, and published in such manner as said Common Council may direct. Report to Common Council.

SEC. 13. Whenever the receipts of said Board, from water rates, or other sources, shall accumulate so that there shall be a surplus, amounting to a sum of not less than five hundred dollars, not needed for the payment of the current expenses, or the extension of said works, it shall be the duty of the Commissioners, together with the Auditor of said city, who shall be associated with them for that purpose, to invest the same in some safe stocks, or upon other real or personal securities. Such investment shall be made in the name of said Board, and in such manner as to make the same available for the payment of interest and principal of the bonds issued as aforesaid, as soon as may be. It shall be the duty of said Commissioners to pay the interest on such bonds, and as fast as such surplus fund will permit, also the principal, as the bonds become due, as funds for such purpose shall, from time to time, accumulate. The said Commissioners may, when they have funds for that purpose, purchase the bonds so issued as aforesaid, whether the same have become due or not; and in case the said Commissioners shall at any time not have funds on hand sufficient to to meet any of the said bonds at the time when they shall become due, they shall have the right to issue new bonds, for Surplus funds to be invested. Payment of bonds and interest. Purchase of bonds. New bonds may be issued.

such amount, and on such time as they shall deem expedient, in the place of bonds so becoming due as aforesaid; the said old bonds to be canceled in the registry thereof, and the said new bonds to be recorded in the manner hereinbefore provided.

Old bonds canceled and new bonds registered.

Oath of Commissioners.

SEC. 14. Before entering upon the duties of their office, said Commissioners shall each take and file with the City Clerk an oath or affirmation, similar to that provided in the case of other officers of said city.

Materials exempt from execution.

SEC. 15. All materials procured, or partially procured, under a contract with the Commissioners, shall be exempt from execution; but it shall be the duty of the Commissioners to pay the money due for such materials, to the judgment creditor of the contractor, under whose execution such material might otherwise have been sold, upon his producing to them due proof that his execution would have so attached, and such payment shall be held a valid payment on the contract.

Commissioners may be removed.

SEC. 16. Any member of said Board of Commissioners may at any time be removed, by a vote of two-thirds of the members elect of the Common Council of said city, for sufficient cause, and the proceedings in that behalf shall be entered on their journal: *Provided*, That the said Common Council shall previously cause a copy of the charges preferred against the Commissioners sought to be removed, and notice of the time and place of hearing the same, to be served on him ten days, at least, previous to the time so assigned; and in case of such removal, the Common Council shall, at their first regular meeting, or as soon thereafter as may be, appoint some person, being a citizen and a freeholder, to fill such vacancy; and the person so appointed to fill such vacancy, may continue in office for the period his predecessor had to serve.

Copy of charges to be served.

Vacancy to be filled.

Power to enter upon land or water.

SEC. 17. The said Commissioners, and, under their direction, their agents, servants, and workmen, are hereby authorized to enter upon any land or water, for the purpose of making surveys, and to agree with the owner of any property, which may be required for the purposes of this act, as to the amount of compensation to be paid to said owner.

SEC. 18. In cases of disagreement between the Commissioners and the owner of any property which may be required for the said purposes, or affected by any operation connected therewith, as to the amount of compensation to be paid to such owner, or in case any such owner shall be an infant, a married woman, or insane, or absent from this State, the Judge of the Circuit Court of Wayne County may, upon the application of either party, nominate and appoint three disinterested persons to examine such property, and to estimate the value thereof, or damage sustained thereby, and to report thereon to the said court, without delay.

In case of disagreement judge of court to appoint appraisers.

SEC. 19. Whenever such report shall have been confirmed by the Circuit Judge of Wayne County, the said Commissioners shall pay to the said owner, or to such person or persons as the court may direct, the sum mentioned in said report, in full compensation for the property so required, or for the damage sustained, as the case may be, and thereupon the said Commissioners shall become seized in fee of such property so required, and shall be discharged from all claim by reason of any such damage.

Confirmation by judge. Payment. Fee of property.

SEC. 20. And in case of the refusal, by any owner or owners, person or persons, to receive such sums awarded to them, for property required, or damages sustained, then the said Commissioners shall deposit with the City Treasurer the sums so awarded, subject to the draft of said owner or owners, person or persons; and thereupon the said Commissioners shall become seized in fee of such property, so required, and shall be discharged from all claim by reason of any such damage; and said City Treasurer shall keep strict account of all sums so deposited, and shall pay out the same on the drafts of the owner or owners, person or persons, to the credit of whom such moneys may have been deposited.

Payment when refused money to be deposited.

City Treasurer to pay on draft.

Injury to property or pollution of water.

SEC. 21. If any person shall willfully do, or cause to be done, any act whereby any work, materials, or property whatsoever, erected or used within the City of Detroit, or elsewhere, by the said Commissioners, or by any person acting under their authority, for the purpose of procuring or keeping a supply of water, shall, in any manner, be injured, or shall willfully pollute the water, shall be deemed guilty of misdemeanor, and, upon conviction, shall be punished therefor, as other misdemeanors are punished.

Penalty for boring pipe or connecting logs without permission.

SEC. 22. If any person shall, without the authority of said Commissioners, as delegated through any of their agents, perforate, or bore, or cause to be perforated or bored, any distributing pipe, or main log, belonging to the water works of said city, or make, or cause to be made, any connection or communication whatever with the said pipes or logs, every person so offending shall, for each offense, forfeit a sum not exceeding fifty dollars and costs of prosecution, to be recovered in the Mayor's Court of said city, or other court of competent jurisdiction.

Power to extend pipes and construct reservoirs beyond limits of city.

SEC. 23. The said Commissioners, in their discretion, shall have power to extend the distributing pipes and mains, and to construct reservoirs, hydrants, and jets, without the limits of said city; and to regulate, protect, and control such portions of said water works, without the bounds of said city, in and after the same manner that they regulate, protect, and control said works within said bounds.

Commissioners to report to Common Council what sum may be required to pay interest, etc.

SEC. 24. It shall be the duty of said Commissioners, at least thirty days before the time fixed by the ordinance of said city for assessing city taxes, to make a special report to the Common Council of said city, what, if any sum, will be needed by said Commissioners, over and above the revenue of said board, to meet the payment of interest or principal of the bonds issued as aforesaid; and it shall be the duty of the Common Council to raise said amount by a special tax, in the same manner as general taxes, to be designated a

Common Council to raise sum by tax.

water tax; and the said amount shall be paid over to said Board by the Treasurer of said city.

SEC. 25. No one or more of the said Commissioners shall be interested, either directly or indirectly, in any contract entered into by them, with any other person; nor shall they be interested, either directly or indirectly, in the purchase of any material to be used or applied in and about the uses and purposes contemplated by this act. Commissioners not to be interested in contracts or purchases of materials.

SEC. 26. All lands, lots, docks, buildings, machinery, pipes, logs, hydrants, and all fixtures whatsoever, purchased, designated, or used for the present water works of the said City of Detroit, are hereby conveyed to and vested in said Board of Commissioners, who shall have full power to regulate, protect, and control the same; and all the authority, rights, and power heretofore exercised and had by said city, over said works, are hereby continued to and vested in said Board of Commissioners. Lands, etc., of present works conveyed to Board of Commissioners.

SEC. 27. The said Commissioners are hereby invested with full power to make and enforce such by-laws, regulations, and ordinances as may be necessary to carry into effect the object and intent of this act, and to supply any power or mode not already specified therein, and shall cause all such by-laws, regulations, and ordinances to be entered into a book to be kept for that purpose, and signed by the President and Secretary, which, when so entered and signed, shall be evidence in any court of justice. Power to make by-laws, etc. By-laws, etc., to be entered in a book.

SEC. 28. All acts, or parts of acts, contravening the provisions of this act, are hereby repealed. Acts repealed.

SEC. 29. This act may at any time be altered, repealed, or amended. Act amended.

Approved February 14, 1853.

**AN ACT to authorize the Water Commissioners of the City of Detroit to loan money for the purpose of extending and improving the Water Works of said City.**

SECTION 1. *The People of the State of Michigan enact*, That the Board of Water Commissioners of the City of Detroit shall have power to loan, upon the best terms they can make, and for such time as they shall deem expedient, a sum of money not exceeding two hundred and fifty thousand dollars, upon the credit of said City of Detroit, and shall have authority to issue bonds pledging the faith and credit of said city for the payment of the principal and interest of said bonds; which bonds shall issue under the seal of said Board of Commissioners, and shall be signed by them, or a majority of them, and bearing interest not exceeding eight per cent. per annum. And it shall be the duty of said Commissioners to cause to be kept an accurate register of all bonds issued by them, showing the number, date, and amount of each bond, and to whom the same was issued; and it shall also be their duty to cause to be furnished to the Auditor of said city a copy of such register, as soon as the same is made, which shall be preserved by said Auditor, and copied into the record of said city. And the said sum of money shall be expended by said Commissioners solely for the purpose of extending and improving the Water Works of the City of Detroit.

This act shall take effect immediately.

Approved February 6th, 1855.

AN ACT to authorize the Water Commissioners of the City of Detroit to borrow money for the purpose of extending and improving the Water Works of said City.

SECTION 1. *The People of the State of Michigan enact*, That the Board of Water Commissioners of the City of Detroit shall have power to borrow, upon the best terms they can make, and for such time as they shall deem expedient, a sum of money not exceeding two hundred and fifty thousand dollars, upon the credit of said City of Detroit, and shall have authority to issue bonds, pledging the faith and credit of said city for the payment of the principal and interest of said bonds; which bonds shall issue under the seal of said Board of Commissioners, and shall be signed by them, or a majority of them, and bearing interest not exceeding eight per cent. per annum; and it shall be the duty of said Commissioners to cause to be kept an accurate register of all bonds issued by them, showing the number, date, and amount of each bond, and to whom the same was issued; and it shall also be their duty to cause to be furnished to the Controller of said city a copy of such register, as soon as the same is made, which shall be preserved by said Auditor, and copied into the records of said city; and the said sum of money shall be expended by said Commissioners solely for the purpose of extending and improving the Water Works of the City of Detroit: *Provided*, That the said Board of Commissioners shall not contract said loan until they are authorized and empowered so to do by the Common Council of the City of Detroit.

Board of Water Commissioners may borrow money.

Money, how expended.

Proviso.

This act shall take effect and be in force from and after its passage.

Approved February 10th, 1857.

**SCHOOL LAWS** of the City of Detroit, as collated and published by the Board of Education of said city, A. D. 1855.*

Detroit to be one school district.

SECTION 1. *Be it enacted by the Senate and House of Representatives of the State of Michigan*, That the city of Detroit shall be considered as one School District, and hereafter all schools organized therein, in pursuance of this act, shall, under the direction and regulations of the Board of Education, be public and free to all children residing within the limits thereof, between the ages of five and seventeen years, inclusive. [*Act of* 1842.

Schools free to scholars of certain ages.

School Inspectors to be elected.

SEC. 2. In lieu of the School Inspectors now required to be elected in said city, there shall be twelve† School Inspectors to be elected in the manner following: at the next annual charter election, there shall be elected in each ward of said city, two School Inspectors, one of whom shall hold his office for two years, and the other for one year; and at every annual charter election thereafter, there shall be elected in each ward, one School Inspector, who shall hold his office for two years. No School Inspector shall be entitled to receive any compensation for his services. [1842.

Their term of office.

Not to receive compensation.

Vacancy in office of School Inspector, how filled.

SEC. 3. In case of a vacancy in the office of School Inspector, the Common Council of the City of Detroit may fill the same, until the next annual election, when, if such vacancy happen in the first year of the term of said office, the electors of the proper ward may choose a suitable person to fill the remainder of such term: *Provided*, The City Clerk shall give notice of such vacancy prior to such election, as may be required in other cases. [1842.

Proviso.

---

* The Figures at the end of each section refer to the year in which the several acts were passed.
For the laws relating to the "colored children" of the city, see Session Laws of 1841, page 48.

† By the increase in the number of wards of the city, the number of School Inspectors has been increased to twenty.

SEC. 4. Every person elected to the office of School Inspector, who, without sufficient cause, shall neglect or refuse to serve, shall forfeit to the Board of Education for the use of the library, the sum of ten dollars, to be recovered in an action of debt in some competent court: *Provided*, No person shall be compelled to serve two terms successively; and the said Board shall make all necessary rules and regulations relative to its proceedings, and punish by fine, not exceeding five dollars for each offense by any member of the Board, who may, without sufficient cause, absent himself from any meeting thereof, to be collected as they may direct.

Persons elected School Inspectors refusing to serve, may be fined.

Proviso.

Board may establish rules and regulations and fine its members.

SEC. 5. The School Inspectors, together with the Mayor and Recorder of said city, (who are declared to be *ex officio* School Inspectors,) shall be a body corporate, by the name and style of "The Board of Education of the City of Detroit," and in that name may be capable of suing and being sued, and of holding and selling, and conveying real and personal property, as the interest of said Common Schools may require; and shall also succeed to, and be entitled to demand all moneys and other rights belonging to or in possession of the Board of School Inspectors, or any member thereof, or any real and personal property or other rights, of any such district in said city; and the clear proceeds of all such property which may come into the possession of said Board, as last aforesaid, shall be expended and disbursed by and under the authority of said Board of Education, for the support of said schools, after paying all just and legal demands existing against the several school districts heretofore existing in said city: *Provided*, That said Board shall not be liable to pay an aggregate amount of indebtedness against any one district, greater than the amount received from the same by said Board. [1842, 1843, 1846.

Who to constitute Board of Education.

Board a body corporate.

Its powers and privileges.

How proceeds of property received by Board to be disposed of.

Proviso.

SEC. 6. The Board of Education (six members whereof may form a quorum,) may meet, from time to time, at such place in said city as they may designate. They may elect one of their own number President, and in the absence of

What a quorum of Board,

the President at any meeting, a majority of the inspectors present may chose one of their number President *pro tem.* [1842, 1846.

Board to elect a President.

Who to be Clerk of Board.

SEC. 7. The Clerk of the said city shall be *ex officio* Clerk of said Board, and shall perform such duties as the Board of Education may reasonably require. In case of the absence of said Clerk, or for any other cause, the Board may choose some suitable person to perform his duties, either as principal or deputy Clerk. [1842.

Recorder of Detroit may meet with the Board.

SEC. 8. The Recorder of said city shall be entitled to a seat at the meeting of said Board, for the purpose of deliberation, and of acting on committees, but shall have no vote therein. [1842, 1846.

General powers and authority of the Board.

SEC. 9. The Board of Education shall have full power and authority, and it shall be their duty, to purchase school-houses, and apply for and receive from the County Treasurer or other officer, all moneys appropriated for primary schools and district library of said city, and designate a place where the library may be kept therein. The said Board shall also have full power and authority to make by laws and ordinances relative to taking the census of all children in said city between the ages of four and eighteen years; relative to making all necessary reports and transmitting the same to the proper offices, as designated by law, so that said city may be entitled to its proportion of the primary school fund; relative to visitation of schools; relative to the length of time schools shall be kept, which shall not be less than three months in each year; relative to the employment and examination of teachers, their powers and duties; relative to regulation of schools and the books to be used therein; relative to the appointment of necessary officers, and prescribe their powers and duties; relative to anything whatever that may advance the interests of education, the good government and prosperity of common schools in said city, and the welfare of the public concerning the same. [1842, 1850, 1855.

May make by-laws and ordinances relative to certain matters.

SEC. 10. The Mayor's Court shall have jurisdiction of all suits wherein the said Board may be a party, and of all prosecutions for violation of said by-laws and ordinances. [1842.

Mayor's Court to have jurisdiction under by-laws of the Board.

SEC. 11. The said Board shall annually, in the month of February, publish in some newspaper of the city, a statement of the number of schools in said city, the number of pupils instructed therein the year preceding, the several branches of education pursued by them, and the expenditures for all things authorized by this act, during the preceding year. [1842.

Board to publish an annual statement.

SEC. 12. The Board of education shall establish a district library, and, for the increase of the same, the Common Council are authorized annually to lay a tax on the real and personal property within said city of a sum not exceeding two hundred dollars, which tax shall be levied and collected in the same manner as the moneys raised to defray the general expenses of said city.* [1842.

To establish a library. The People ex rel., vs. the Treasur'r Wayne Co. 8 Mich. 392.

Tax for, how levied.

SEC. 13. The Common Council of said city are hereby authorized, once in each year, to assess and levy a tax on all the real and personal property in said city, according to the city assessment rolls of that year, which shall not exceed two dollars for every child in said city, between the ages of four and eighteen years, the number of children to be ascertained by the last report on the subject, on file in the office of the Clerk of the County of Wayne, or in the office of the Secretary of said Board of Education, and certified by the President thereof; and the said tax shall be collected in the same manner as the moneys raised to defray the general expenses of said city. All said money shall be disbursed by the authority of said Board for the maintenance and support of said schools, and for no other purpose. The said Board of Education shall have authority to establish a high school in said city, and also to appoint a Superintendent of the public schools, under the charge of said Board, with such salary and

Com. Council may levy taxes for support of schools.

How taxes collected and disbursed.

Board may establish high school, and appoint a Superintendent of public schools.

---

*As to fines for library, R. S. 1846, Chap. 158, secs. 25, 26.

with such powers and duties as shall be prescribed by said Board of Education. [1855.

Who to be Treasurer of Board. His duties.

SEC. 14. The Treasurer of said city shall be the Treasurer of said Board, unless otherwise directed by said Board; he shall keep all moneys belonging to said schools separate from the moneys belonging to the corporation of said city, and he shall not pay out or expend the school moneys without the authority of the said Board. [1842.

Duty of Collectors relative to school moneys.

SEC. 15. The Collector of said city, when he shall have paid any school money to said Treasurer or other person, shall take a receipt therefor, and file the same with the Clerk of said Board; and it shall be the further duty of the Collector, when he shall have made his final return concerning the collection of said tax, to make a report to said Board, stating the whole amount of school tax, the amount collected, and the amount returned by him to the Common Council as unpaid or uncollected. If any Collector shall neglect or refuse to pay to said Treasurer the sums of money required by his warrant, or to account for the same as unpaid, at the time and in the manner required by law, the Recorder of the city of Detroit, or the President of the Board of Education of said city, shall forthwith issue a warrant under his hand, directed to the Sheriff of said county, commanding him to levy such sums as shall remain unpaid and uncounted for, together with his fees for collecting the same, of the goods and chattels, lands and tenements of such Collector and his sureties, and to pay the same to the Treasurer of said Board of Education, and return such warrant within twenty days after the date thereof. [1855.

Collectors refusing to pay moneys collected, how proceeded against.

Collectors and Treasurer to give bonds.

SEC. 16. The Controller and Treasurer shall, before they enter on their duties under this act, enter into such bonds to said Board, and with such sureties as may be deemed necessary, conditioned for the faithful discharge of their duties respectively under this act.* [1842.

---

* See sec. 1 of act of 1846, cited on the next page, for further provisions relative to bond of collectors.

SEC. 17. All parts of acts, so far as they relate to the City of Detroit, inconsistent with this act, are hereby repealed. And it shall not be necessary to elect any school district officers in said city, as heretofore required by law. [1842.

Prior acts repealed.

SEC. 1. That all taxes which have been or may hereafter be assessed and levied by the Common Council of the city of Detroit, under and by virtue of the authority conferred on said Council by the thirteenth section of an act entitled "An act relative to Free Schools in the city of Detroit," shall be set forth in the assessment roll of said city, in a separate column, apart and distinguished from all other city taxes; and that the Collector of said city shall collect and is hereby authorized and required to collect, said taxes in money, and said Collector shall not be required or permitted to receive in payment of said taxes any liabilities or evidences of debt against said city. [1843.

School taxes to be placed in separate column on assessment roll.

What Collector shall receive for school taxes.

SEC. 1. That the Collectors of the City of Detroit, elected in the different wards of said city, shall act as Collectors of the school tax assessed and levied in said city, in their respective wards, under and by virtue of the provisions of the act to which this act is amendatory; and that each of said Collectors, previous to his entering upon his duties, shall, in addition to the bond now required by law, make and execute to the Board of Education of said City of Detroit a bond, with two good and sufficient sureties, to be by them approved, in the penal sum directed by said Board, conditioned for the faithful performance of his duties as such Collector; and that in case of neglect or refusal of any one of said Collectors to execute and obtain such bond according to the provisions of this section, he be subject to a penalty of one hundred dollars, to be collected in an action of debt, which may be brought in any court in this State, at the suit and in the name of the said Board of Education of the City of Detroit. [1846.

Who to collect school taxes.

Collectors to give bonds.

Conditions of bonds.

SEC. 1. That in addition to the taxes mentioned in the act to which this act is amendatory, the Common Council of the

Taxes for building sch'l houses and purchasing lots therefor may be levied.

City of Detroit is hereby authorized and empowered to levy and collect a tax, not exceeding fifteen hundred dollars in any one year, to be expended in the purchase of lots in said city, for the use of the public schools thereof, and in the erection and building a school house or school houses, with the necessary outbuildings and fixtures, on any lot or lots which may be so purchased, or any other lots now owned by the Board of Education of said city, or which the said board may hereafter acquire: *Provided*, That said tax, when so levied and collected, shall be paid to the Treasurer of said Board of Education, and be vested in said board to and for the purpose hereinbefore stated, and no other, and also that the title to such lots purchased shall also be in said board, for the purpose aforesaid. [1847.

Proviso.

Title to school lots in whom vested

Freemen to vote on taxes for school houses.

SEC. 2. Said tax shall not be levied or collected, unless at a meeting of the freemen of said city, called for such purpose, as hereinafter provided; a majority of the freemen present shall assent to the same. [1847.

Mayor or Recorder to call meeting of freemen to vote on taxes

SEC. 3. It shall be the duty of the Mayor, or Recorder, in case of the absence of the Mayor, or a vacancy in his office, to call such a meeting of the freemen of said city, for the purpose of giving their assent or dissent to such tax, when it shall be requested by petition, signed by twenty-four freemen of said city; which call shall particularly express the object of such meeting, and shall be published in two of the daily newspapers published in the said City of Detroit, one week previous to such meeting: *Provided*, That the Mayor may call such meeting upon the notice herein mentioned, without such petition, at his own option. [1847.

Proviso.

Meeting of freemen may be called by two memb'rs of Council in certain cases.

SEC. 4. If the said Mayor or Recorder shall refuse to call such meeting, upon the presentation to either of them of such petition, or shall neglect to do so for three days after the presentation of such petition, any two members of the Common Council of said city may, on the like petition, call such meeting, upon a like notice and publication thereof, in the manner and for the time hereinbefore specified in the case of a call by the Mayor or Recorder. Such meeting may be adjourned, from time to time, by vote of a majority of those present. [1847.

SEC. 5. The said tax shall be levied and collected in the same manner as the tax provided for in the thirteenth section of the act to which this act is amendatory, and shall be consolidated therewith on the tax rolls; but it shall be the duty of the said Board of Education, in each and every year, when such tax is levied and collected, to separate the amount thereof from the gross amount of money received by said Board, for such year, and set it apart as a fund to be reserved for the purposes specified in the first section of this act. [1847. How taxes for school houses and lots to be collected.

SEC. 6. The Board of Education of the City of Detroit is hereby authorized, from time to time, on such term or terms of payment as they may deem proper, to borrow a sum of money not exceeding in all the sum of five thousand dollars, for the purposes specified in the first section of this act, at a rate of interest not exceeding seven per cent. per annum, payable semi-annually, and to issue the bonds of said Board in such form, and executed in such manner, as said Board may direct: *Provided*, That said Board shall issue no bond for a less sum than fifty dollars. [1847, 1850. Board of Education may borrow money and issue bonds for payment. Proviso.

SEC. 7. The bonds issued under this act shall be a charge upon all the property of said Board, which shall constitute a security for the payment thereof: *Provided*, That no legal proceedings shall be instituted to enforce such lien, or to sell any property of said Board for the payment of the principal money of any of said bonds, until one year after such principal shall become due, according to the tenor and effect thereof. [1847. Bonds to be a lien on property of Board. Proviso.

SEC. 8. It shall be the duty of the Board of Education, whenever they shall borrow any money, under the provisions of this act, annually to appropriate a sufficient sum out of any money which may come into their hands, to pay the Board to keep interest on bonds paid and provide sinking fund to pay principal.

interest upon the same; and also in addition thereto, an annual sum equal to five per cent. upon the amount so borrowed, to be invested, under the direction of said Board, in bonds of the City of Detroit, bearing interest at such prices as the same can be purchased, to accumulate as a sinking fund for the payment of the principal of the sum so borrowed; both of which appropriations shall take precedence of all others. [1847.

Removal of School Inspector from ward for which he is elected not to vacate his office.

SEC. 3. The removal of any member of the Board of Education of the City of Detroit, from the ward for which he is elected School Inspector, after such election, shall not operate to vacate his office; but notwithstanding such removal, any Inspector, so removing, shall continue to hold his said office, and to be a member of said Board, and all provisions of any act or acts, which make such removal a vacation of said office, are hereby repealed: *Provided*, The removal of such member shall not be from the city. [1850.

Proviso.

Persons paying school taxes in any district may send scholars to the schools therein.

SEC. 137. Any person paying taxes in a school district in which he does not reside, may send scholars to any district school therein, and such person shall, for that purpose, have and enjoy all the rights and privileges of a resident of such district, except the right of voting therein, and shall be rated therein for teachers' wages and fuel, and in the census of such district, and the apportionment of moneys from the school fund, scholars so sent, and generally attending such school, shall be considered as belonging to such district: *Provided*, That a majority of the qualified voters attending at any regular meeting in the district in which such person resides, shall have determined that no school shall be taught in said district for the year: *Or, Provided, further*, That such person shall not reside in any organized school district. [*Revised Statutes* 1846, *page* 235, *and S. L.* 1850.

Proviso.

**AN ACT to amend an Act entitled "An Act in relation to Free Schools in the City of Detroit," approved February 7th, 1857.**

SECTION 1. *The People of the State of Michigan enact,* That in lieu of the fifteen hundred ($1,500) dollars mentioned in the first (1) section of an act approved March twelfth, (12,) eighteen hundred and forty-seven, (1847,) and in addition to all other taxes, authorized by law to be assessed and levied for school purposes in the City of Detroit, the Common Council of said city is hereby authorized and empowered to levy and collect a tax not exceeding twenty thousand ($20,000) dollars in any one year, to be expended in the purchase of lots, and in paying for lots already purchased in said city for the use of the public schools thereof, and in the erection and building of school houses with the necessary outbuildings and fixtures, on any lots now owned by the Board of Education, in said city, or which said board may hereafter require. Said tax, when so levied and collected, shall be paid to the Treasurer of said Board, and shall vest in said board for the sole purposes hereinbefore stated, unless the said board shall, by resolution, direct the same to be applied in whole or in part for the maintenance and support of the schools of said board, in which case said tax may be so applied; said tax shall be collected in the same manner, and with the same right, duties, powers, and obligations, as the general school taxes in said city.

Common Council authorized to levy taxes for building school houses.

Tax to be paid to treasurer of Board of Education.

SEC. 2. This act is ordered to take immediate effect.

Approved March 7, 1861.

---

NOTE.—The State School money must be distributed on the first Monday in May in each year —*R. S.* 233, *Section* 119, *S. L.* 1847.

**AN ACT to incorporate the Fire Department of the City of Detroit.**

Preamble. *Whereas*, The members of an association, known as the "Fire Department of the City of Detroit," have petitioned the Legislature to grant them an act of incorporation, to enable them the more effectually to accomplish the objects of their organization, and to provide means for the relief of disabled firemen and their families: Therefore,

Fire Department of Detroit a body corporate. SECTION 1. *Be it enacted by the Senate and House of Representatives of the State of Michigan*, That all persons who now are, or may hereafter become members of the Fire Department of the City of Detroit, and their successors, shall be, and hereby are ordained, constituted, and declared to be, and continue a body politic and corporate, in fact and in name, under the name and style of "The Fire Department ot the City of Detroit," for the purposes recited in the above preamble, and by that name they and their successors may and shall have perpetual succession, and shall be known in law, capable of suing and being sued, of pleading and being impleaded, of answering and being answered unto, of defending and being defended, in all suits, complaints, matters, causes, courts, and places whatsoever, and both in law and equity; and capable of having a common seal; of acquiring, by purchase, gift, devise, or otherwise; and of holding and conveying any real, personal, or mixed estate, necessary, proper, or expedient, for the objects of this incorporation: *Provided*, That the amount of said estate shall at no time exceed the sum of thirty thousand dollars.

May have a seal and hold real estate.

Proviso.

May make by-laws, etc. SEC. 2. The members of the Fire Department of the City of Detroit, hereby incorporated, shall have, and are hereby declared to have, full power and authority to make and prescribe such by-laws, rules, ordinances, and regulations, and the same to alter, amend, and change at pleasure, as to them, from time to time, shall seem needful or proper, touching the management and disposition of their funds for the objects aforesaid; touching the regular and special meetings of the department; the regulation, duty and conduct of their members, delegates, and Board of Trustees; the election and displacing of officers and delegates; the admission and expulsion of members; the filling of vacancies in offices; and touching every other matter and thing necessary or expedient for the good government and promotion of this incorporation, or which appertains to the business and objects for which the said incorporation is, by this act, instituted: *Provided*, That such by-laws, rules, ordinances, and regulations be not repugnant to the constitutional laws of the United States, or of this State.

Relative to disposal of funds. Meetings. Conduct of members and officers. Election of same. Admission and expulsion of members. Filling vacancies, etc.

Proviso.

SEC. 3. The officers of said department, by this act incorporated, shall be a President, Vice President, Secretary, Treasurer, and Collector, who, together with the Chief Engineer of the Fire Department, and the delegates from the several fire companies, and other bodies, pursuant to the provisions of the constitution and by-laws of the department, shall constitute a board of trustees, a majority of whom shall be a quorum for the transaction of business; and said officers and delegates, separately, and as a board of trustees, shall do and perform such duties and things as may be incumbent upon, or required of them, by the constitution or by-laws of the department.

Officers of Department.

Board of Trustees.

SEC. 4. There shall be an annual meeting of the members of said corporation on the third Monday of January in each year, at which the officers shall be elected by ballot, by a majority of the members present, from their own body. And the officers elected shall hold their offices for one year, or until others be chosen in their places; but in case it at any time happens that an election of officers shall not be made or had on that day, the said corporation shall not be dissolved, but it shall and may be lawful to hold such election

Annual meeting of Fire Department.

thereafter, pursuant to public notice given in one or more of the newspapers printed in said city.

Names of officers for first year.

SEC. 5. Of the Fire Department of the City of Detroit, Robert E. Roberts shall be President; Frederick Buhl, Vice President; Edmund R. Kearsley, Secretary; Darius Lamson, Treasurer; and Elijah Goodell, Collector; who, together with the Chief Engineer of the Fire Department, duly appointed by the Common Council of the City of Detroit, and the delegates chosen as aforesaid, shall constitute the first Board of Trustees, and shall hold their offices until the third Monday of January next, or until others shall be chosen in their stead.

Interest of funds appropriated to relief of indigent and disabled firemen and their families.

SEC. 6. The interest arising from the funds of the said corporation, except sufficient to defray incidental expenses, shall be appropriated to the relief of such indigent and disabled firemen and their families as may be interested in the fund, and who may, in the opinion of a majority of the trustees, be worthy of assistance.

Certificates, how obtained.

SEC. 7. All certificates now required to be obtained by firemen, from the Clerk of said city, pursuant to the provisions of any law of this State, shall hereafter be obtained from the department, by this act incorporated; which certificate, signed by the President and Treasurer of this department, and countersigned by the City Clerk of said city, and under the seal of this incorporation, shall have the like effect of those heretofore obtained from the said City Clerk, and shall be satisfactory evidence of the facts therein contained. And each person applying for such certificate, shall pay therefor such sum as the by-laws of the department shall prescribe, for the benefit of the corporation, and the objects thereof.

Their effect.

List of members to be made out yearly and given to City Clerk.

SEC. 8. It shall be the duty of the Board of Trustees to make out and deliver to the City Clerk, once in each year, or whenever he may request it, an accurate list of all the members of this corporation, who are exempt from jury or military duty, that they are, or may become, entitled to the benefits thereof.

SEC. 9. This act is hereby declared to be a public act, and the same shall, in all courts and places, be regarded benignly and favorably for every beneficial purpose hereby intended. This is a public act.

SEC. 10. The Legislature may alter, modify, amend, or repeal this act, by a vote of two-thirds of each House. May be repealed or modified.

SEC. 11. All acts and parts of acts which contravene the provisions of this act, are hereby repealed; and this act shall take effect from and after its passage. Acts inconsistent herewith, repealed.

Approved February 14, 1840.

---

AN ACT to amend an Act entitled "An Act to Incorporate the Fire Department of the City of Detroit," approved February 14, 1840.

SECTION 1. *The People of the State of Michigan enact*, That section one of an act entitled "An Act to incorporate the Fire Department of the City of Detroit," be, and the same is hereby, amended, by striking out the word "thirty," in the last line, and inserting the word "sixty," so that said section shall read as follows:

SEC. 1. *Be it enacted by the Senate and House of Representatives of the State of Michigan:* That all persons who now are, or hereafter may become, members of the Fire Department of the City of Detroit, and their successors, shall be, and hereby are, ordained, constituted, and declared to be and continue, a body corporate and politic, in fact and in name, under the name and style of the "FIRE DEPARTMENT OF THE CITY OF DETROIT," for the purposes recited in the above preamble; and by that name they and their successors may and shall have perpetual succession, and shall be known in law, capable of suing and being sued, of pleading and being impleaded, of answering and being answered unto, of defending and being defended, in all suits, complaints, matters, causes, courts, and places whatsoever, and both in law and equity; and capable of having a common seal; of acquiring by purchase, gift, devise, or otherwise, and of holding and conveying any real, personal, or mixed estate, necessary, proper, or expedient for the object of this incorporation: *Provided*, That the amount of said estate shall at no time exceed the sum of sixty thousand dollars.

Approved February, 1859.

---

# POLICE COURT ACT.

AN ACT to establish a Police Court in the City of Detroit, approved April 2d, 1850.

Police Justice. SECTION 1. *Be it enacted by the Senate and House of Representatives of the State of Michigan*, That there shall be a Police Justice in the City of Detroit. The first election for said Justice shall be held on the first Monday of May next, in the City of Detroit, to be conducted in the same manner as justices of the peace are elected at the charter election of said city; and the first incumbent of said office shall hold his office from the time he is elected till the fourth Election. day of July, in the year 1854; and at the charter election of said city and the interval of every four years, the said Justice shall be elected in the manner provided for the election of Justices of the Peace in said city, to hold his office for four years, the term of which shall commence on the fourth day of July of the year in which he is elected; and in case of a vacancy occuring in the said office of police justice, the Common Council shall order a special election, giving twenty days' notice thereof. And the said Police Justice shall, before Oath. entering upon the duties of his office, take and subscribe the oath prescribed by the constitution of this State, before some officer authorized by law to administer oaths, and deposit the same with the Clerk of the County of Wayne, who shall file and preserve the same in his office.

SEC. 2. He shall, except in case of his absence, or inability to act, have sole and exclusive jurisdiction to hear all complaints, to conduct all examinations in criminal cases, and to try all offenses which by the laws of this State are now brought and established within the jurisdiction of justices of the peace, and which may hereafter arise within the corporate limits of said city of Detroit. Powers and duties.

SEC. 3. Warrants may be issued in criminal cases for the apprehending of offenders by any justice of the peace in said City of Detroit; but they shall be made returnable before the said Police Justice, except in case of his absence or inability, or a vacancy in said office. Ibid.

SEC. 4. He shall reside and keep an office in the city of Detroit, and attend to all complaints of a criminal nature which may be brought before him at all reasonable hours, and in case of his removal from said city, his death or resignation, his office shall be vacated, and another person then acting in said city as a justice of the peace, shall be appointed by the Common Council of said city, who shall serve as such Police Justice until after the next ensuing charter election, when a Police Justice shall be elected to fill the vacancy. Ibid. Vacancy.

SEC. 5. No justice of the peace residing in said city of Detroit, shall be entitled to receive any fees for, or bound to render any services in criminal cases, except during the sickness, absence or inability of the said Police Justice as aforesaid; in which case it shall be the duty of the several justices of the peace in said city, to render the same services, and they shall receive the same fees, as though this act had not passed. Justices of the Peace.

SEC. 6. When any warrant returnable before said Police Justice shall be returned during his absence, sickness, or Warrants.

inability to act on during a vacancy (if such occurs) in said office, any further proceedings on such warrant may be had before any justice of the peace residing in said City of Detroit; and all warrants issued by the said Police Justice for the apprehending of criminals, shall have the same effect and be subject to the same restrictions as warrants issued by justices of the peace in similar cases.

Security for costs.

SEC. 7. The said Police Justice shall have authority in all cases, at his discretion, either before or after the issuing of process, to require of the complainant security for costs, to the satisfaction of said justice; and the person giving such security shall sign a memorandum, in writing, to that effect, which said justice shall keep as a part of the record of the case; and in all cases non-resident complainants shall give such security before process shall issue. If the defendant or prisoner be discharged on examination by said Police Justice, or acquitted on trial, the said justice shall enter a judgment for costs against the surety and the complainant, either or both of them, which shall be of like force and effect, and shall be collected on execution as any other judgment rendered by a justice of the peace: *Provided*, That said justice shall certify on his record that such payment of costs by the prosecutor or his surety in his opinion, is equitable; and all costs collected by him from either parties to complaints or prosecutions before him and which by law are taxable as justices' costs, shall be accounted for and paid over to the County Treasurer of the County of Wayne, as often as once in every thirty days, and his receipt taken for the same; and all fines or other moneys coming to his hands, shall be paid out and disposed of as is now provided by law with reference to justices of the peace.

Proviso.

Salary.

SEC. 8. The said Police Justice shall not be entitled to receive to his own use any fees for services performed under this act, but in lieu thereof he shall receive an annual salary of twelve hundred dollars per year for the time he shall exercise the duties of such office, to be fixed from year to year by the Board of County Auditors for said County of Wayne, which shall be allowed, raised, and paid by said board as other county charges are allowed and paid; and during the time he remains such Police Justice he shall not perform the duties of a civil magistrate.

SEC. 9. This act shall take effect and be in force from and after its passage; but nothing in this act contained shall be so construed as in anywise to affect the jurisdiction of justices of the peace in criminal proceedings, until said Police Justice shall be elected and qualified according to the provisions of this act.

SEC. 10. The said Police Justice shall have power to appoint a clerk for said court, who shall receive no fees for his services, but in lieu thereof an annual salary of five hundred dollars, payable quarterly from the County Treasury of Wayne County, under the direction of the Board of Auditors for said county. (*See note D.*)

---

**AN ACT to amend an Act entitled "An Act to amend an Act entitled 'An Act to revise the Charter of the City of Detroit,' approved February 5th, 1857," approved March 12th, 1861.**

SECTION 1. *The People of the State of Michigan enact*, That section seventeen of an act entitled "An Act to amend an act entitled 'An Act to revise the Charter of the City of Detroit,' approved February 5th, 1857," approved March 12th, 1861, be, and the same is hereby amended, so as to read as follows:

SEC. 17. That section eighteen be amended so as to read as follows: The Collector for each ward shall collect all State and county taxes assessed and imposed upon the real and personal property of such ward, and such city, highway, sewer and school taxes, as shall be placed in his hands for col- Ward Collectors, duties of.

NOTE D.—This section was added by the Act of February 17th, 1857.

lection by the Receiver of Taxes, or other proper officer of said city, and shall account for and pay over the same as required by law, or by ordinance or resolution of the Common Council of said city. The Director of the Poor and Constables shall have the power, and perform the duties of such township officers elected under the general laws of the State, subject to the provisions of this act.

Director of Poor and Constables, duties of. Smith vs. People, Sup. Court, April Term, 1861.

SEC. 2. This act shall take immediate effect.

Approved May 10, 1861.

[For section amended, see *ante*, p. 31.]

# APPENDIX.

---

AN ACT to establish the Detroit House of Correction and authorize the confinement of convicted persons therein.

SECTION 1. *The People of the State of Michigan enact*, That the building erected for that purpose by the City of Detroit, shall be known and recognized as the "Detroit House of Correction," and shall be used for the confinement, punishment and reformation of criminals, or persons sentenced thereto, under the provisions of this act, or any law of this State authorizing the confinement of convicted persons in said House of Correction.

Name of.

How to be used.

SEC. 2. The management and direction of the said House of Correction, subject to periodical inspection by the State authorities in their discretion, shall be under the control and authority of a Board of Inspectors to be appointed for that purpose by the Common Council of the City of Detroit, but the chairman of the Board of Inspectors of the State Prison and the Mayor of said city, shall, by virtue of their office, be members of said Board of Inspectors, who, together with three persons to be appointed on the nomination of the Mayor by the Common Council of said city, shall form said board. The term of office for the appointed members of said board, shall be three years; but the members first appointed, shall hold their office respectively as shall be determined by lot at the first meeting of said board, for one, two and three years, and thereafter one member shall be appointed each year for the full term of three years.

How controlled.

Board of Inspectors, how appointed.

Term of office.

To adopt rules and regulations.

SEC. 3. The said Board of Inspectors is hereby authorized and empowered to establish and adopt rules for the regulation and discipline of said House of Correction, and upon the nomination of the Superintendent thereof, to appoint the subordinate officers, guards and employees thereof, to fix their compensation and prescribe their duties generally, to make all such by-laws and ordinances in relation to the management and government thereof as they shall deem expedient. But no order, ordinance, resolution or act of said Board, fixing the salary or compensation of any officer or employee of said institution, shall be binding and valid until it shall have received the sanction of the Common Council of said city, by a vote of a majority of all the aldermen elect in said city, at some regular meeting subsequent to the meeting on which such proposed salary or compensation shall have been presented to said Common Council, and no appropriation of money shall be made by the said Board of Inspectors for any purpose other than the ordinary and necessary expenses and repairs of said institution, except with the sanction of said Common Council as provided in the case of salaries and compensation of officers and employees.

Officers: how appointed.

Salary of officers, Common Council to sanction.

Expenditures, how made.

Meetings of Board, when.

SEC. 4. Said inspectors shall serve without fee or compensation. There shall be a meeting of the entire Board at the House of Correction once in each year, at such time as shall be fixed by said Board. One or more of said appointed inspectors shall visit the said House of Correction once, at least, in each month. There shall be a meeting of said appointed inspectors at said House of Correction once in every three months, when they shall fully examine into its management in every department, hear and determine all complaints or questions not within the province of the superintendent, to determine and make such further rules and regulations for the good government of said House of Correction, as to them shall seem proper and necessary. All rules, regulations or other orders of said Board, shall be recorded in a book to be kept for that purpose, which shall be deemed

Meetings at House of Correction, when; to examine into manageme't; to hear complaints.

Records of.

a public record, and with the other books and records of said House of Correction, shall be at all times subject to the examination of any member or committee of the Common Council, the Controller, Treasurer, or Attorney of said city, or any officer or person duly authorized by any court of record in this State, to make such examination.

Open to inspection.

SEC. 5. The books of said House of Correction shall be so kept as to clearly exhibit the state of the prisoners, the number received and discharged, the number employed as servants, or in cultivating and improving the premises, the number employed in each branch of industry carried on, and the receipts from, and expenditures for, and on account of each department of business, or for improvement of the premises. A quarterly statement shall be made out, which shall specify minutely all receipts and expenditures, from whom received, and to whom paid, and for what purpose, proper vouchers for each, to be audited and certified by the inspectors and submitted to the Controller of said city, and by him to the Common Council for examination and approval. The accounts of said House of Correction shall be annually closed and balanced on the first day of January of each year, and a full report of the operations of the preceding year, shall be made out and submitted to the Common Council of said city, a copy of which shall be transmitted to each department of the State Government, and to each county in the State having contracts with said city for the confinement and maintenance of convicted persons, and such report shall be published in some newspaper published in the city, or in such other form as shall be directed by the Common Council.

Books of, how kept.

Statements, when to be made, and what to show

Accounts, how audited.

Annual report.

How published.

SEC. 6. The Common Council of said city may require such further reports and exhibits of the condition and management of such institution as to them shall seem necessary and proper, and may, with the approval of the Mayor and Inspectors, for misconduct or willful neglect of duty and upon sufficient evidence thereof, remove any officer or employee,

Employees, how removed.

or inspector of said institution, except the superintendent thereof, who shall be removable for the causes, and as provided in the charter of said city. But any subordinate officer or employee may be removed by the superintendent at his discretion, or by the Board of Inspectors with the approval of the Superintendent.

Superintendent, his powers and duties.

SEC. 7. The Superintendent of the said House of Correction shall have entire control and management of all its concerns, subject to the authority established by law and the rules and regulations adopted for its government; it shall be his duty to obey and carry out all written orders and instructions of the inspectors not inconsistent with the laws, rules and regulations relating to the government of said institution. He shall be responsible for the manner in which said House of Correction is managed and conducted. He shall reside at said House of Correction, devote his time and attention to the business thereof, and visit and examine into the condition and management of every department thereof and of each prisoner therein confined, daily, or as often as good order or necessity may require. He shall exercise a general supervision and direction in regard to the discipline, police and business of said House of Correction. The deputy superintendent of said House of Correction shall have and exercise the powers of the superintendent, in his absence, so far as relates to the discipline thereof and the safe keeping of prisoners.

Residence of.

Deputy Superintendent his powers and duties.

Counties may contract for keeping of criminals.

SEC. 8. The Board of Supervisors of any organized county of the State shall have full power and authority, to enter into an agreement with the Common Council of the City of Detroit or with any authorized agent or officer in behalf of said city, to receive and keep in the Detroit House of Correction any person or persons who may be sentenced to confinement by any court or magistrate in any of said counties for any term not less than sixty days. Whenever such agreement shall have been made, it shall be the duty of the Board of Supervisors for any county in behalf of which such agreement

Notice of contract, how given.

shall have been made, to give public notice thereof in some newspaper published within said county, and in case no paper is published in said county, then such notice shall be published in some newspaper within the judicial district to which said county is attached, for a period not less than four weeks, and such notice shall state the period of time for which such agreement will remain in force.

Duty of courts and justices in counties making contract.

SEC. 9. In every county having such agreement with the said City of Detroit, it shall be the duty of every court, police justice, justice of the peace, or other magistrate, by whom any person for any crime or misdemeanor, not punishable by imprisonment in the State Prison, may be sentenced for any term not less than sixty days, to sentence such person to the Detroit House of Correction, there to be received, kept and employed, in the manner prescribed by law, and the rules and discipline of the said House of Correction; and it shall be the duty of any such court, police justice, justice of the peace, or other magistrate, by a warrant or commitment duly issued by the court, justice or magistrate declaring such sentence, to cause such person so sentenced, to be forthwith conveyed by some proper officer to said House of Correction.

Duty of Sheriffs and Constables in counties making contract.

SEC. 10. It shall be the duty of the sheriff, constable, or other officer in and for any county having such agreement with said city of Detroit, to whom any warrant or commitment for that purpose may be directed by any court or magistrate in such county, to convey such person so sentenced, to the said Detroit House of Correction and there deliver such person to the keeper or other proper officer of said House of Correction, whose duty it shall be to receive such person so sentenced, and to safely keep and employ such person for the term mentioned in the warrant or commitment, according to the laws of said House of Correction, and the officer thus conveying and so delivering the person or persons so sentenced, shall be allowed such fees or compensation therefor as shall be prescribed or allowed by the Board of

Fees of officers.

Supervisors for the county in which such person shall have been convicted.

State Prison Inspectors may contract for confinement of criminals.

SEC. 11. The inspectors of the State prison may contract with the said City of Detroit, or any duly authorized agent or officer in behalf of said city, for the confinement and maintenance, in the Detroit House of Correction, of persons convicted of any offense punishable by imprisonment in the State prison : *Provided*, That the compensation to be paid for such confinement and maintenance, shall not exceed the sum of one dollar per week; and upon the completion and execution of any such contract, the Inspectors of the State Prison and of the said House of Correction shall give public notice thereof, in some weekly newspaper, in each county in which a weekly newspaper is published, after which any male person, under the age of twenty-one years and above the age of sixteen years, who shall be convicted of any offense, murder and treason excepted, punishable by imprisonment in the State prison, may, in the discretion of the court before whom such conviction shall be had, be sentenced to imprisonment in the Detroit House of Correction; and every male between the ages of sixteen and twenty-two years, who shall, for the first time, be so convicted, shall be sentenced to said Detroit House of Correction. And every female, who shall be so convicted, shall be sentenced to said House of Correction. And every person so sentenced shall be received into the said House of Correction, and shall be kept and employed in the manner prescribed by law, and shall be subject to the rules and discipline of said House of Correction.

Compensat'n

Notice of contract, how given.

Duty of Sheriffs.

SEC. 12. It shall be the duty of the Sheriff of any county within which any person shall be convicted and sentenced, as in the eleventh section of this act provided, to convey such person to the said House of Correction, and deliver him or her to the superintendent thereof, for which such sheriff shall be paid the same fees and compensation allowed for conveying persons to the State prison.

Fees of.

SEC. 13. All provisions of law authorizing the commitment and confinement of males under sixteen, and females under fourteen years of age, in the jails, work-houses or houses of correction in the City of Detroit, are hereby made applicable to all persons who may or shall be, under the provisions of this act, sentenced to the said Detroit House of Correction.

Expenses of House of Correction, how defrayed.

SEC. 14. The expenses of maintaining the said House of Correction, over and above all receipts for the labor of persons confined therein, and for the support of those whose support shall not be chargeable to the County of Wayne, or be otherwise provided for, shall be audited and paid, from time to time, by the Common Council of the City of Detroit, and shall be raised, levied and collected as part of the ordinary expenses of said city.

Inspectors to make certificates; where filed and upon whom served.

SEC. 15. Whenever the said House of Correction shall, in the opinion of the Board of Inspectors, by this act created and established, or a majority of them, be so far completed as to insure the safe confinement and employment therein, of persons intended to be therein confined, they shall make duplicate certificates thereof under their hands and seals, one of which they shall file in the office of the Clerk of Wayne County, and the other shall be served upon the Sheriff of said county, and the said Sheriff shall thereupon transfer all such persons to the said House of Correction, and the Superintendent thereof shall receive such persons and safely keep them for the term for which they are sentenced, and employ them according to the discipline and rules established for the government of said House of Correction.

Certificate to be published.

SEC. 16. Immediately after filing the certificate of completion as aforesaid, the said Inspector shall cause a copy thereof to be published in at least three newspapers published in said county, and thereafter it shall be the duty of every court or magistrate in the said County of Wayne, authorized by law to sentence or commit any person to the county jail of said county as vagrants, common drunkards, disorderly

What offenders from Wayne Co. to be confined in.

persons, common prostitutes, or for assault and battery, petit larceny, or other offenses punishable by imprisonment in the county jail, or by virtue of any final sentence of conviction except for contempt, to sentence such person to be confined in the said House of Correction, there to be received, kept and employed according to law under the rules and regulations of said House of Correction. *Duty of officers to convey prisoners to.* And it shall be the duty of all officers having the execution of the final process of any court or magistrate sentencing convicted persons to said House of Correction, to cause such convicts to be conveyed forthwith to said House of Correction, and such officer or officers shall be paid therefor, the fees allowed by law for conveying persons to the county jail. *Fees of officers.* *Exception.* But this section shall not apply to those juvenile offenders, who, by law, may be sent to the reform school at Lansing.

*Power to sentence vagrants to House of Correction.*

SEC. 17. It shall be lawful for any justice of the peace, police justice, or other magistrate having jurisdiction thereof, in the County of Wayne, or in any other county, having an agreement with the City of Detroit, for the confinement and maintenance of convicted persons in said House of Correction in all cases of complaint for vagrantcy to commit any person except such juvenile offenders as are mentioned in the last preceding section, convicted on such complaint before such justice or magistrate to said House of Correction for a term not exceeding six months.

*Escape or breaking House of Correction with intent, etc.*

SEC. 18. Every person lawfully committed to said House of Correction, who shall escape from or break said House of Correction with intent to escape therefrom, or who shall attempt by any force or violence, or in any other manner to escape from said House of Correction, whether such escape be effected or not, shall, upon conviction thereof, *Penalty.* be punished by confinement in said House of Correction for a term not exceeding double the term for which he or she was so sentenced, to commence from and after the expiration of his or her former sentence.

Females in State Prison may be transferred for remaind'r of term.

SEC. 19. Upon the completion and execution of a contract for the confinement and maintenance of persons liable to imprisonment in the State prison, in the said House of Correction, as provided in section eleven of this act, it shall be competent and lawful for the Inspectors of the State prison to transfer to said House of Correction all females confined in the State prison, and such persons so transferred shall be received into said House of Correction, and there confined and employed for the unexpired term of their sentences, respectively.

Record of infractions o rules to be kept.

Sec. 20. The Superintendent of said House of Correction shall cause to be kept a record of each and all infractions of the rules and discipline of said House of Correction, with the names of the convict or convicts offending, and the date and character of each offense, and every convict sentenced for one or more years whose name does not appear upon such record, shall be entitled to a deduction of three days per month from his or her sentence for each month they shall continue to obey all the rules of the said House of Correction.

Reward for good behavior.

# REGISTRY LAW.

---

AN ACT further to preserve the purity of Elections, and guard against the abuses of the Elective Franchise, by a Registration of Electors, approved February 14, 1859.

Registration ordered.

SECTION 1. *The People of the State of Michigan enact*, That there shall be, in the year one thousand eight hundred and fifty-nine, a registration of the qualified electors of the State. The Aldermen of every incorporated city, and the Supervisor, Treasurer, and Clerk of every township, shall constitute a Board of Registration for such city or township, and their duties shall be as follows: They shall, respectively, provide suitable bound books, or registers, one for each township, and one for each ward, so made and arranged as to contain an alphabetical list of the respective books, names, christian or baptismal, and surnames, in full, of all persons declared by the Constitution of the State to be electors and entitled to vote, residing in their townships or wards, and the date of the registration; and, if the elector resides in a city, or incorporated village, also his residence by the number of the dwelling and the name of the street, if any, and if none, a description of the locality of the same.

Board of Registration.

Board to provide books; how arranged and what to contain.

## REGISTRATION IN CITIES.

City boards to publish notice of meeting of board.

SEC. 2. Each city board shall, at least two weeks previous to the time of their meeting, in each ward, cause to be published in one or more newspapers printed and published in such city, a notice that the Board of Registration will meet on the first Monday of October, in the year one thousand eight hundred and fifty-nine, at nine o'clock in the fore-

Time and place of meeting designated.

noon, to make a perfect list, as near as may be, of all persons residing in such ward, qualified as electors, under the constitution; and designating the place in each ward where said board will meet for that purpose. And they shall also cause handbills to be posted in at least twenty conspicuous places in each ward, containing a similar notice of the time and place of such meeting of the board for that ward, which notice shall also contain a true copy of section one of article seven of the constitution, relative to the qualifications of electors. And the board may so divide and classify themselves, that two or more of them may be assigned to different wards, the more speedily to complete the registration; and in case of the sickness or absence of any Alderman, or his inability or refusal to serve at the session, in any ward, the board shall, in writing, under the hand of their chairman, immediately appoint the Assessor of the ward, or any Justice of the Peace, to act in his stead, who shall be, for the purposes of registration in that ward, deemed a member of the Board of Registration. They shall continue in session not less than three, nor more than five days, in each ward. All necessary blanks and instructions to aid the board in the discharge of their duties, and all other expenses in performing the same, including the employment of printers, for printing such notices, and the registry lists, shall be provided by the board, and be paid for by the city.

Handbills to be posted.

What notice to contain.

Vacancies in board.

Length of session.

Expenses, how paid.

SEC. 3. At the time and place mentioned in such notice, the board, or those members thereof so classified and assigned for that ward, shall meet and proceed to the registration in such book, which book shall be called the *Register of Electors*, for such ward, of the names of persons at the time residing in such ward, and so qualified as follows, to wit: Their sessions shall be public, and during the first two days thereof, they shall not write in the register the name of any person, without a request made by him personally, and in their presence; but shall allow him, if able and willing so to do, to write his own name therein, in the proper place.

Duty of board.

Sessions to be public.

Registration, how made. In case of such request, the name of the elector shall be plainly written, by a member of the board, who shall also note his residence, as required by section one of this act. After the first two days of the session, it shall be the duty of such board to proceed to complete the list, by writing in such register, the names of all the remaining residents of the ward, known by them to be such, and to be qualified as aforesaid, with the proper descriptions above mentioned; but they shall, during their whole session, permit any such qualified person, residing in the ward, whose name has not already been entered in the register, to write it there himself. Opposite to every name, on such register, shall be noted by the board the day and year of its entry, and during such session, and all future sessions of the board, in any city or township, they may, for their better information in making the registration, have before them the poll list of the next preceding general election, charter election, or township meeting, to be returned to the proper keeper, at the close of the session, and all such entries shall be made with ink. Board may question and require applicants to make oath. The board, at every session, shall have power, and it shall be their duty to question every person presenting himself for registration, touching his residence and other qualifications, as an elector of the ward, and it shall be the duty of the applicant to make truthful answers to all such questions, and the board may, for the more perfect examination of the applicant, swear, and employ an interpreter, truly and impartially to interpret all such questions and answers, and if the applicant Penalty for making false statement. shall, in his answers, make any material statement which is false, he shall, upon conviction thereof, pay a fine of not more than one hundred nor less than five dollars, and be imprisoned in the county jail not more than thirty nor less than five days.

What persons not entitled to register. SEC. 4. The name of no person but an actual resident of the ward at the time of the registration, and entitled under the constitution, if remaining such resident, to vote at the then next general or charter election, shall be entered in the register. Neither the board, nor any member thereof, shall write or enter in the register the name of any person, nor suffer him to write or enter his name therein, whom they know, or have good reason to believe, not to be such resident and so qualified; nor shall any person, knowing or having good reason to believe himself not to be such resident, and so qualified, write his name therein, or cause it to be done; and every person so offending shall, upon conviction, be punished for each offense by a fine of not more than five hundred nor less than twenty-five dollars, and be imprisoned in the county jail not more than ninety nor less than ten days. Penalty for fraudulent registration.

## REGISTRATION IN CITIES AFTER 1859.

SEC. 5. On the Thursday, Friday, and Saturday next preceding the general election, and on the Thursday and Friday next preceding the day of the regular charter election of the city, and during the two days (Sundays excepted) which next precede any special election, after the year one thousand eight hundred and fifty-nine, the Board of Registration of the city, to be constituted as aforesaid, shall be in session at such places in the several wards as they shall designate in their notices, to be published and posted up as hereinafter provided, from nine o'clock in the forenoon until five o'clock in the afternoon, for the purpose of completing the lists of qualified voters, during which session it shall be the right of each and every person then actually residing in the ward, and who at the then next approaching election may be a qualified elector, and whose name is not already registered, to have his name entered in the register, which shall be done in the manner above described; and such board, and each member thereof, and each applicant for registration, is hereby vested and charged with the same rights, powers, duties, and penal liabilities, touching the examination of applicants, as hereinbefore provided. Time for registration in cities after 1859.

Notice to be given.

SEC. 6. At least two weeks previous to the commencement of any such session, the board, at the expense of the city, shall cause a notice thereof to be printed and published in one or more newspapers published in such city, designating the place of holding the same; and shall also cause the same notice to be printed in handbill form, and posted up in at least ten conspicuous places in each ward; which handbill shall also contain a true copy of the list of names then appearing in the register for the ward. And immediately after the close of the polls of such election, the Clerk of the Board of Inspectors of that election, and before the counting of the votes, shall, under the direction and by the assistance of the Inspectors, insert and write upon, or attach to such printed handbill, all the names of electors appearing on the register, and not on such handbill, so that such handbill, so corrected, shall be a true copy of the list then appearing in such register, and shall, with the Inspectors, or a majority of them, certify and sign such copy, and file the same in the office of the County Clerk, who shall carefully keep and preserve the same; and the same shall be evidence, *prima facie*, of the original; and in case of the loss or destruction of the original, the same or a certified copy thereof shall be used in its stead.

What notice shall contain.

Duty of inspectors.

List to be filed with City Clerk.

SEC. 7. At the close of their sessions, the board, or the members who made the registration in the particular ward, shall sign the list, adding the date of their signature, and shall immediately deposit the same for safe keeping with the City Clerk, who shall carefully preserve the same in his office until delivered, as hereinafter provided.

Registers to be delivered to inspectors, when.

SEC. 8. At any such general, special, or charter election, in the city, and as soon, at least, as the poll in each ward is opened, the City Clerk shall cause the proper register to be placed in the hands of the Inspectors of Election, to be used by them during the same, and returned to the City Clerk immediately thereafter. And they shall not receive the vote of any person whose name is not written therein; but if any person shall offer and claim to vote at such election, whose name is not so registered, his name may be registered by the Clerk of the Election, under the direction of the Inspectors, upon the same terms and conditions hereinafter prescribed for the like cases, arising at elections in townships, substituting *ward* for *township;* and both the applicant and the qualified elector shall be subject to the same penalties prescribed in cases so arising.

Name may be registered on day of election.

### REGISTRATION IN TOWNSHIPS.

SEC. 9. It shall be the duty of the Board of Registration in each township, to wit: The Supervisor, Treasurer, and Clerk thereof, and in case of the absence of any of them, or his inability to serve, the Justice of the Peace, not holding the office of Supervisor or Town Clerk, whose term of office will first expire, to provide, at the expense of the township, the like book for their township, for the purpose of the like registration of the qualified electors thereof, to be arranged in the same manner, save that in cases where the elector does not reside within the limits of an incorporated village, a description of his residence may be omitted; but in case he resides within such limits, and in the township, a description of his residence, by the street, and the number of the dwelling, or other brief but intelligible method; and the names of such resident electors of the village shall be written in said register, in a list separate and distinct from those of other electors of the townships, so as to exhibit a correct registration for the village, which list shall be called the *Village Election Register.*

Registration in townships, who to constitute board.

Books, how arranged.

### REGISTRATION IN TOWNSHIPS IN 1859.

SEC. 10. At the annual meeting of each township, on the first Monday of April, in the year one thousand eight hundred and fifty-nine, the Township Treasurer shall, at a place as near as practicable to that of the meeting, and of

Proceedings at township election in 1859.

convenient access to the electors, have said book or register in readiness for the entry of their names, and each qualified elector, residing in the township, may then write his name, at length, in the proper place in said register, if able and willing to do so, or the Treasurer shall, upon request made in his presence, by the elector personally, write the name of such elector in its proper place. And in all cases, under this act, the board, or the members thereof, receiving or making the entry of a name, shall note, or cause to be noted, the day and year thereof. During such township meeting, and during all future sessions of the board, the township poll list of the next preceding general election or township meeting, shall be before him or them for their better information in making the registration, to be returned to the Clerk at the close of the meeting or the session. The Supervisor, or other person or persons charged by law with the assessment of property in the township, for the purpose of State taxation, shall, while making such assessment, and in connection with the performance of that duty, in the year one thousand eight hundred and fifty-nine, have with him the said register, and shall allow each qualified elector, residing in the township, whose name has not been entered therein, to write the same, or shall himself, at the like personal request of the elector, write the same therein, at the proper place, and shall, after completing his valuation of property, and on or before the first day fixed by law for reviewing his assessment, deposit said register with the Township Clerk, who shall carefully keep and preserve the same in his office.

Board to have access to township poll list.

Supervisor to register names while making assessments.

Registration after 1859, how made.

SEC. 11. After the year one thousand eight hundred and fifty-nine, it shall be the right of any such qualified elector, residing in the township, and entitled to vote at the next election therein, and whose name has not been registered, on any day except Sunday, the days of the session of the Board of Registration, and the days intervening between them and the next approaching election, to apply to the Township Clerk, in person, for the registration of his name, and if, upon such examination as is required by the next following section of this act, the Clerk shall be satisfied that such applicant is a resident of the township, and otherwise qualified and entitled to vote in such township, at the then next election, to be held therein, the name of such applicant shall be written, either by himself or the Clerk, upon a separate paper, to be kept by the Clerk, his residence described, and the date of the entry noted, as required in the two last preceding sections; which paper shall be laid before the Board of Registration of each township, at its next meeting for examination and review. And the names of such persons, appearing thereon, as the board shall be of opinion are qualified electors at the then next election, and entitled to vote thereat, may, by some member of the board, and under their direction, be entered in the proper register, in the manner above set forth. And every applicant to the Clerk, so causing his name to be entered upon such separate paper, knowing or having good reason to believe himself not to be such resident, and qualified to vote in such township at the then next election, shall, upon conviction thereof, be punished by fine and imprisonment, as provided in the thirteenth section of this act. Penalty for fraudulent registration.

REGISTRATION IN TOWNSHIPS AFTER 1859.

Sec. 12. On the Saturday next preceding the general election, the annual township meeting, and preceding any special election, after the year one thousand eight hundred and fifty-nine, the Board of Registration of each township shall be in session at the office of the Township Clerk, from nine o'clock in the forenoon, until five o'clock in the afternoon, for the purpose of completing the list of qualified electors; during which session it shall be the right of each and every person who, at the next approaching election, or township meeting, may be a qualified elector and entitled to vote thereat, and whose name is not already registered, to Sessions of township boards, when held.

have his name duly entered on said register, which shall be done in the manner above set forth. The board shall have the power, and it shall be their duty, and the duty of the Clerk, and of the Supervisors individually, when acting under this statute, to question every person presenting himself for registration, touching his residence, and his other qualifications as an elector of the township; and it shall be the duty of the applicant to make truthful answers to all such questions. And the Board, Supervisor, Clerk, or Treasurer, as the case may be, may, for the more perfect examination of the applicant, swear, and employ an interpreter truly and impartially to interpret such questions and answers. And if any such applicant shall, in his answers, make any material statement which is false, he shall, upon conviction thereof, pay a fine of not more than one hundred dollars, nor less than five dollars, and be imprisoned in the county jail not more than thirty nor less than five days.

Powers and duties.

Penalty for false statement.

Sec. 13. The name of no person but an actual resident of the township, at the date of the registration, and entitled under the constitution, if remaining such resident, to vote at the then next election or township meeting, shall be entered in the register. Neither the board, nor any member thereof, shall write, or enter therein, the name of any person, nor suffer him to write or enter his name therein, whom they know, or have good reason to believe not to be such resident and so qualified; nor shall any person, knowing or having good reason to believe himself not to be such resident, and so qualified, write his name therein; and every person so offending shall, upon conviction, pay for each offense a fine of not more than five hundred nor less than twenty-five dollars, and be imprisoned in the county jail not more than three months, nor less than ten days.

Who not entitled to register.

Penalty for fraudulent registration.

Sec. 14. At such election, or township meeting, and as soon, at least, as the poll is opened, the Township Clerk shall cause the register to be placed in the hands of the Inspectors

Clerk to deliver register to inspectors on day of registration.

of Election, to be used by them during the election, and to be returned to the Clerk, immediately thereafter; and they shall not receive the vote of any person whose name is not written therein. But in case any person shall offer and claim the right to vote, whose name is not so registered, his name may then be registered by the Clerk, under the direction of the Inspectors, upon the terms and conditions following: One of the Inspectors shall administer to him an oath, in the following form, viz: You do solemnly swear that you will true answers make to such questions as shall be asked you, touching your qualifications as an elector at this poll, so help you God; or an affirmation to the same effect, which oath or affirmation, if he be unable to understand the English language, may be interpreted to him by an inspector, or interpreter, sworn by an inspector, which interpreter shall also interpret his answers to the Inspectors. If, in his answers, on oath, he shall state positively that he has resided in the township ten days next preceding said election, designating particularly the place of his residence, and that he possesses the other qualifications of an elector, under the constitution, stating such qualifications; and shall, furthermore, swear that, owing to the sickness or bodily infirmity of himself, or of some near relative, residing in the same household, (giving the name of said relative,) or owing to his absence from the township, on public or official business, or his own business, and without intent to avoid or delay his registration, during the then last session of the board, he has been prevented from causing his name to be previously registered; and if, furthermore, some qualified elector of the township, and not a candidate for any office, at that election, shall take an oath before said Inspectors, which oath any one of them may administer, that he is well acquainted with such applicant, that he has, in fact, resided in the township ten days previous to such election, and that he, the freeholder, [qualified elector,] has good reason to believe, and does believe, that all the statements of such applicant are true, the In-

Names may be registered on election day.

spectors may, in their discretion, direct the Clerk to register his name in the proper place, with the proper date; and if such applicant or such qualified elector shall, in said matter, willfully make any false statement, he shall be deemed guilty of perjury, and, on conviction, be subject to the pains and penalties thereof.

Penalty.

Vote may be challenged.

SEC. 15. Any person offering to vote at any such election, in a city, township, or village, whose name is not written in the proper register, may be objected to, and his vote challenged, for that cause, by any elector present, and entitled to vote at that poll; and on such challenge being made, the Inspectors shall, if on inspection, they find his name not so written in the proper register, refuse the vote. But nothing in this act contained, shall be held or construed in any way to affect or impair the right of any inspector or elector to challenge any person offering to vote, nor the effect of such challenge, as now established by law, or as such right and such effect may hereafter be established: *Provided, however*, That the vote of no person shall be received whose name is not so registered.

Proviso.

Penalty for illegal voting

SEC. 16. Any person, knowing that his name is not so registered, who shall vote, or offer to vote at any such election, either in a city or township, and every Inspector, knowing such name not to be so registered, willfully and corruptly consenting to receive such vote, shall, if the vote be received by reason of such consent, be, for every such offense, punished as above provided, in section thirteen of this act; and on the trial of the person so voting or offering to vote, the presumption shall be that he knew that his name was not so registered.

Actual residence a condition of registration.

Penalty.

SEC. 17. The name of no person shall be registered in any township or ward where he does not actually reside at the time of the registration; and every person who shall willfully register, or cause or procure, by enticements, or other means, the name of any person to be registered contrary to the provisions of this act, shall, upon conviction of any such offense, be also punished as above provided, in section thirteen of this act.

## DEATH AND REMOVAL OF ELECTORS.

SEC. 18. At every session of the Board of Registration of any township or ward, after the year one thousand eight hundred and fifty-nine, it shall be their duty to review the list of names in their register, and if it shall have come to their knowledge that any person whose name has been registered has died or has removed therefrom and ceased to reside therein, they shall place the letter D against the name of the deceased person, and the letter R against the name of the person who has so removed, with the date of the entry and the initials of the name of the member making it, so as to show by whom and when made, and thereafter such name shall be considered and treated as no longer in the list, and shall be omitted in the copies above provided for. But if it shall happen that such entry was erroneously made, and such person shall thereafter appear at any election and claim the right to vote thereat, his name may, on his application, be again registered, but upon the following terms: he shall, upon his oath or affirmation, which any member of the board of inspectors, or the board of registration may administer, declare that he has not removed from, but is still a resident of the township or ward, and is otherwise a qualified elector, and entitled to vote. And on making such oath or affirmation, his name may be registered in the manner above described, either by the board of registration or the board of inspectors. And if such applicant shall swear or affirm falsely, he shall be liable to the pains and penalties of perjury. But in case such entry shall be made falsely, maliciously, and without credible information, the member of the board making it shall be deemed guilty of a misdemeanor and be punished as such, and the party aggrieved shall be entitled to recover of him in an action on the case trible dam-

Board to review and correct lists.

Provisions for subseq'nt registration.

Conditions.

Penalty.

Penalty for false entry.

ages for the injury, and trible costs of suit in any court having jurisdiction of the cause, and the record of the defendant's conviction of the criminal offense, duly authenticated, shall be *prima facie* evidence of his liability.

Copy of township register to be furnished by Township Clerk.

SEC. 19. It shall be the duty of any city or township clerk, except during the session of the board or on days of election, on the demand of any qualified elector of the ward in such city, or of such township, on payment or tender of his legal fees, to make out, certify, and at his office deliver to such elector a true copy of the contents of the register of election of such ward or township; for which he shall be entitled to receive at the rate of fifty cents for every one hundred names.

Penalty for destroying register.

SEC. 20. Whoever shall willfully cut, burn, mutilate, or destroy any such register of electors, or copy thereof filed for preservation, or shall unlawfully take and carry away the same, or unlawfully conceal or refuse or neglect to surrender the same, with intent to prevent its being used as authorized by law, shall be deemed guilty of larceny; and whoever shall falsify any such register or copy, by unlawfully erasing or obliterating any name or entry lawfully made therein, or by unlawfully inserting therein any name, note or memorandum, with intent thereby to influence or affect the result of any election, or to defraud any person of an election to office, shall be deemed guilty of forgery; and the person so offending shall for every such offense, be punished by imprisonment in the State Prison not more than five years, or by a fine not exceeding five hundred dollars, and imprisonment in the county jail not more than one year, nor less than ninety days.

Penalty for falsifying register.

Township Clerk to file copies with County Clerk and Township Treasurer.

SEC. 21. To the end that the contents of such registers may not be lost, it shall be the duty of every township clerk, within twenty days after each general election, to make, certify and transmit to the county clerk of the proper county, and also to the township treasurer, a true copy of such contents, to be by such county clerk and township treasurer filed and preserved in his office; for which, when received, he shall give such township clerk a receipt; and such township clerk shall be entitled to receive therefor from the township at the rate of fifty cents for every one hundred names; and such copy, or a copy thereof, certified by the county clerk or township treasurer, shall be *prima facie* evidence of the contents of the original, and in case of the loss or destruction of the original, shall be used in its stead.

Fees.

Copy evidence.

## VILLAGE ELECTION.

SEC. 22. It shall be the duty of the President and Trustees of every incorporated village, or the persons who are by law authorized to make by-laws and charged with the general powers to regulate and control the municipal affairs of the village, to procure from the Clerk of the township or of the townships, respectively, within which said village may wholly or in part lie, and it is hereby made his duty to furnish to them, at the expense of the village, from the register of electors of the township or townships within which such village is situated, a true copy of the village election register, to be certified by such Township Clerk, and to be delivered to the Inspectors of Election in such village, and used for the purpose of the village election, in the same manner and to the same effect as is above provided for the general election and township meetings in townships, as near as may be; and there are hereby given to the Inspectors of any such village election the same power and authority, and to applicants for registration the same rights and privileges which are given to township inspectors and to applicants at township elections, respectively, at such elections; and such inspectors and applicants and other persons mentioned in the foregoing provisions regulating elections in townships, are charged with the same duties and subjected to the same penalties and liabilities as are provided in like cases at such elections in townships; and the vote of no per-

Village elections. Duty of President and Trustees.

son shall be received whose name is not written in such register, or in the copy thereof used by the Inspectors of the Election. Such copy of the village register shall be furnished at least ten days before the first village election in the year one thousand eight hundred and sixty, and as often as once in two years thereafter, and oftener if the proper municipal authority shall require it; and the township clerk shall be entitled to receive therefor at the rate of fifty cents for every one hundred names.

Voting under assumed name.

SEC. 23. If any person falsely personating any qualified elector whose name is registered, shall at any election vote, or offer to vote, in the name of such elector, or if any person shall knowingly encourage or persuade any such person to vote or offer to vote, or if any person assuming a false or fictitious name, shall vote or offer to vote by that name, or shall enter or cause to be entered upon the register as his own a false name, the person so offending shall, for every such offense, be punished as above provided in section twelve of this act.

Penalty.

What courts to have jurisdiction.

SEC. 24. The Recorder's Court in the City of Detroit shall have cognizance and jurisdiction of all offenses under this act committed within the limits of said city, and the offender may in all cases be there proceeded against by information, as provided by the charter of said city, or any other statute applicable thereto. In all other cases the Circuit or District Court for the proper county shall have cognizance of such offenses committed within the county; and in cases where the punishment is by such fine or such imprisonment, one or both, as a justice's court may impose, the proper justice's court shall have cognizance and jurisdiction thereof.

Violation of duty a misdemeanor.

SEC. 25. Any willful violation of duty by any person charged with the execution of this act or any provisions thereof, not herein particularly provided for, shall be deemed a misdemeanor, and the person guilty thereof shall be punished accordingly. And it is hereby made the duty of every circuit and district court in its charge to the grand jury, to

Duty of Courts and Prosecuting Attorneys.

call their special attention to the necessity of making diligent and careful inquiry touching offenses arising under this act; and also, the duty of every prosecuting attorney whenever he shall receive credible information that any such offense has been committed, to cause the same to be prosecuted.

SEC. 26. It shall be the duty of every City Clerk and Township Clerk, annually, in the month of November, to forward by mail to the Secretary of State, at the seat of government, the aggregate number of names, not marked with the letter D or R, appearing in the register for such city or township, omitting the names; and the Secretary of State is hereby required to keep a record thereof in such manner as to show the number of votes in such city and township, arranged in alphabetical order, in a book to be kept for that purpose. And he shall, within twenty days from the approval of this act by the Governor, cause a printed copy of the same to be forwarded by mail, to every such City and Township Clerk in the State. Report to Secretary of State. Duty of Secretary of State.

SEC. 27. Each member of a city board of registration, while acting under this act, shall be entitled to receive two dollars a day, for every day he shall actually serve in performing his duties, to be paid by the city; and each member of a township board shall receive the same compensation as now provided for Inspectors of election. Compensation.

SEC. 28. Each member of a board of registration shall, before he enters upon the discharge of his duties under this act, make and subscribe the oath of office contained in the first section of article eight of the constitution.

SEC. 29. Every register shall be of good paper, well bound and arranged alphabetically in the following form as near as practicable: Registers, in what form arranged.

| DATE. | NAME. | RESIDENCE. | REMARKS. |
|---|---|---|---|

This act shall take effect immediately.

AN ACT to amend an act, entitled "An Act further to preserve the Purity of Elections and guard against the abuses of the elective franchise by a registration of electors," approved February 14, 1859.

SECTION 1. *The People of the State of Michigan enact*, That on the second Thursday, Friday and Saturday next preceding the general election, and on the second Thursday and Friday next preceding the day of the regular charter election of the City of Detroit and not afterward, the Board of Registration shall be in session at such places in the several wards and districts as they shall designate in their notices as prescribed by law, from nine o'clock in the forenoon until five o'clock in the afternoon, for the purpose of completing the list of qualified voters in pursuance of said act, approved February 14th, 1859, and any member of said board may administer an oath or affirmation to the applicant, that he shall true answers make to all questions put to him touching his qualification as an elector.

SEC. 2. So much of sections one and five of the act aforesaid, approved February 14th, 1859, as may be inconsistent with this act, and all other acts and parts of acts contravening the provisions of this act, are hereby repealed: *Provided*, That this act shall apply and have force only in the City of Detroit, in the County of Wayne.

# INDEX.

26

## ERRATUM.

In section 16, page 142, the word "*Controller*" should read "COLLECTOR."

www.ingramcontent.com/pod-product-compliance
Lightning Source LLC
LaVergne TN
LVHW011212110826
845150LV00006B/1412

* 9 7 8 1 4 2 5 5 1 7 2 3 6 *